Rails in the Dales

Eight Yorkshire Railways

David Joy

RAILWAY & CANAL HISTORICAL SOCIETY

First published 2017
by the Railway & Canal Historical Society

www.rchs.org.uk

The Railway & Canal Historical Society was founded in 1954
and incorporated in 1967.
It is a company (no.922300) limited by guarantee
and registered in England as a charity (no.256047)
Registered office: 34 Waterside Drive, Market Drayton TF9 1HU

ISBN 978 0 901461 65 0

Designed and typeset by
Malcolm Preskett
Printed and bound in Great Britain by
Short Run Press, Exeter

Cover illustrations

Front:
Class 4 No.75019 leaves Swinden Quarry on the Grassington branch
with a ballast train in the summer of 1968. David Rodgers

Back:
Denthead viaduct is crossed by class 47/4 No.47565
heading a diverted West Coast express. Gavin Morrison

Contents

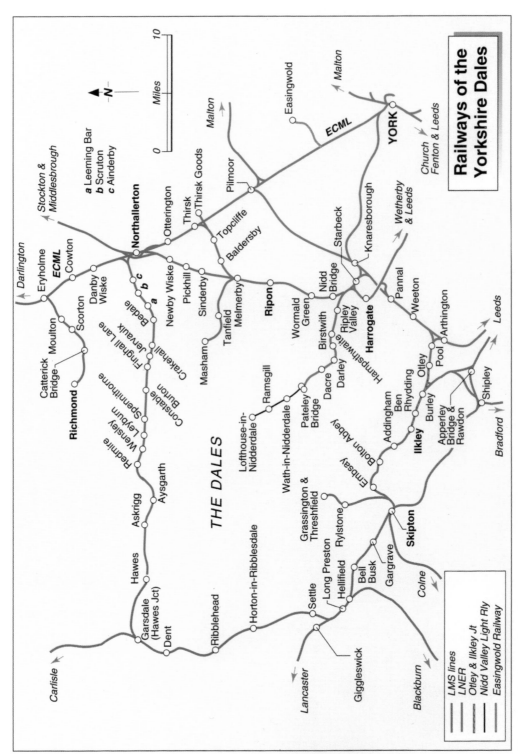

Railways of the Yorkshire Dales

a Leeming Bar
b Scruton
c Ainderby

LMS lines
LNER
Otley & Ilkley Jt
Nidd Valley Light Rly
Easingwold Railway

Map drawn by Roger Carvell

4

Introduction

THERE are hundreds of dales scattered through northern England but only one Dales with a capital 'D'. It is a region in the heartland of Yorkshire with superb scenery as well as one magnificent railway and branch lines mainly past but some still present. Quite what constitutes the Dales has long been imprecise, but in 1954 there came artificial boundaries with the designation of the Yorkshire Dales National Park. These embrace the core landscape, but country with Dales-like qualities extends much further and played a pivotal role in railway development. Thirty years elapsed between completion of the first lines in the region historically regarded as the Dales and any significant railways in the smaller area within what is now the National Park.

The main valleys radiate from the highest mountains like spokes of a wheel so that at no point are the headwaters of their rivers more than 25 miles apart. This book covers eight railways in eight individual dales and looks at them geographically in radial order beginning with Wharfedale. One of its two railways helped to turn Bolton Abbey into a tourist honeypot and the other was the Grassington branch still partially open for mineral traffic. Next come Ribblesdale, Dentdale and Garsdale, linked by the Settle–Carlisle line now enjoying cult status. A branch into Swaledale only reached the gateway town of Richmond but was blessed with a terminus that has few if any equals. Wide and green Wensleydale eventually got a railway through its entire upper reaches from Leyburn and lower down was the separate Masham branch feeding a private reservoir line in lesser-known Colsterdale. Finally and wholly outside today's National Park is Nidderdale, which had both a branch to Pateley Bridge and Bradford Corporation's remarkable Nidd Valley Light Railway.

The genesis of this book was a series of articles in *Backtrack* magazine on railways in Wharfedale, Wensleydale and Nidderdale. Clearly they told less than half the story and much more was required. Above all, coverage of such items as features of each line and its traffic needed to be preceded by an overall chronological account, which is given in the first chapter. It breaks new ground as the two previous books on the subject adopted purely a dale-by-dale approach. Michael Blakemore described his 2001 album as seeking only to provide a pictorial survey. The earlier 1975 work was by K. Hoole, who as a true North Eastern Railway historian scarcely acknowledged the existence of the Midland's Settle–Carlisle railway !

This line's overwhelming improbability and the extraordinary events culminating in its survival could easily make it dominate this book to the exclusion of everything else. The danger has been firmly resisted as it has a vast bibliography. Those wanting to know more and help sustain its future are recommended to join the Friends of the Settle–Carlisle Line (www.foscl.org.uk).

This book is published by the Railway & Canal Historical Society, which has a deserved reputation for fully referenced and erudite academic works. However this book does not pretend to be one of them. Instead it follows the approach preferred by the late David St John Thomas, who edited the Society's recent *How Railways Changed Britain* and who did not favour notations. He wanted a text that would appeal to a broad readership. This is also the aim of *Rails in the Dales* in seeking to show how lines evolved and the affect they had on the communities they served. It accords with the mission statement on the RCHS website of making the study of history something you can enjoy.

In order to avoid the text getting indigestible for the general reader, opening and closure dates are generally given to the nearest month. Exact dates are in the reference section on pages 88 to 91, which also includes an alphabetical list of stations showing when they were opened and closed.

Throughout the text, use is made of imperial measurements rather than metrication, which was unknown to nineteenth-century railway builders. A final point concerns money. To say that something cost say £1,000 in 1850 does not convey a great deal in present-day terms. Money values therefore include today's figure based on the percentage increase in the Retail Price Index. This is a controversial area and it cannot be stressed too highly that it is no more than an approximate indication.

Grateful acknowledgements are due to Michael Blakemore and Barney Trevivian, respectively the publisher and designer of *Backtrack*; Gavin Morrison and David Rodgers for their photographs; Ruth Annison for her help with the Wensleydale Railway; and Malcolm Preskett, who has designed this book and assisted in many other ways.

David Joy
March 2017

Chapter One

Rails in the Dales

North Eastern lines

THE clear front-runner in terms of railways that came anywhere near the Dales was what is now the East Coast main line. Conceived in the mid-1830s, the section from York to Darlington was opened by the Great North of England Railway in March 1841. It passed within ten miles of Richmond, gateway town to Swaledale, and it made eminent sense for the company to obtain parliamentary sanction in 1845 for a branch to the ancient market centre. A prime attraction was rich reserves of lead higher up the dale, which prior to the railway age had to be taken by packhorses and then carriers across to Stockton-on-Tees before it could be loaded into coastal craft. Money supply was cheap, engineering difficulties were few and the branch had the luxury of double track. Diverging from the East Coast main line at Dalton junction (later known as Eryholme junction), five miles south of Darlington, it was quickly built and opened in September 1846.

Hard on its heels should have been similar rail access into Wensleydale. It was now the high noon of the Railway Mania. The heart of the Dales with its high mountains and deep river valleys did not favour railway construction, but countless schemes were nevertheless promoted. Not one succeeded. All that came to pass was a short eight-mile branch from the main line at Northallerton as far as Bedale. Its origins could scarcely have been more tangled and its lack of progress must at the time have caused dismay.

Powers were obtained in June 1846 by the Newcastle & Darlington Junction Railway, now leasing the Great North of England line and forming part of the empire of the infamous George Hudson. A month later the combined concern became the York & Newcastle Railway, which was thus in charge of both the embryo Bedale line as well the Richmond branch on its completion in September. The expanding empire brought a further name change to the York, Newcastle & Berwick Railway in 1847, but the glory years had not long to last. Collapse of the Railway Mania brought construction of

Above: The superb terminus at Richmond, a station in a class of its own. Although not then complete, it was the first to serve the Dales when opened in September 1846. This perspective is thought to be by its architect George Townsend Andrews and was exhibited at the Royal Academy in 1848.
NRM Pictorial Collection/Science & Society Picture Library

Opposite, top: Branches into the Dales built by the North Eastern Railway included the line from Arthington to Otley. It opened in February 1865 and passenger traffic lasted for one hundred years and one month. K4 2-6-0 No.3442 *The Great Marquess* is heading the RCTS Dalesman tour of 4 May 1963 at the intermediate station of Pool-in-Wharfedale. Gavin Morrison

Lower: The Otley & Ilkley Joint Railway represented a rare collaboration between the Midland and North Eastern companies. Services into Ilkley from Leeds and Bradford via Guiseley have unusually seen threatened closure succeeded by electrification. EMU No.308 165 is about to depart from the terminus on 5 October 1995; the former through platforms for Skipton services, now a car park, are on the right. Gavin Morrison

the Bedale branch to a standstill and it was just one of many similar schemes that terminated ignominiously in a field close to the nearest road. In this case it was at Leeming Lane, alongside the A1, reached in March 1848. It was less than two miles from Bedale, but here passengers were forced to transfer to horse-drawn conveyances for the next seven years.

Improved trading conditions at last led to incorporation in August 1853 of the independent Bedale & Leyburn Railway. It was empowered to complete the branch that had been left in abeyance beyond Leeming Lane and then extend it a further 11¾ miles to the sizeable town at the foot of upper Wensleydale. Bedale finally saw its first train in February 1855 and opening of the extension to passengers in May 1856 meant that Leyburn was at last on a

par with Richmond as a key gateway to the Dales with rail access. Two years earlier had seen the formation of the North Eastern Railway, which among numerous other concerns absorbed the York, Newcastle & Berwick Railway. As part of its policy to secure territorial monopoly, it took over the Bedale & Leyburn line in 1859 and thus now controlled both the Richmond and Leyburn branches.

The Mania years produced other important main lines on the edge of the Dales. Cutting across all four of its major east-flowing rivers – the Wharfe, Nidd, Ure and Swale – as they meandered into the Vale of York was the Leeds & Thirsk Railway. Authorised in 1845 and running via both Harrogate and Ripon, it was opened throughout in July 1849 and renamed the Leeds Northern two years later. It too formed part of the North Eastern Railway in 1854, which meant that for the time being a single company had the whip hand with railways serving the Dales.

In 1859 the North Eastern secured powers for a 11½-mile branch extending through Nidderdale from Ripley junction, on the Leeds–Thirsk line north of Harrogate. Terminating at Pateley Bridge, it was opened in May 1862 and became noted for carrying top-quality stone from local quarries.

On the south side of Harrogate, the Leeds–Thirsk line was also the springboard for a railway running up Wharfedale from a triangular junction at Arthington to Ilkley. Sanctioned in 1861, it saw its first trains over the 3½ miles as far as Otley in February 1865. Services into Ilkley began six months later in August and this former village began its transformation into a spa town of national repute. Swaledale, Wensleydale, Nidderdale and Wharfedale now all had their branch lines and matters might well have gone no further in any country blessed with a planned approach to railway development. Only hills and small villages lay beyond their respective termini.

Enter the Midland

PROVIDING a hint of what was to come was the presence in Ilkley of trains operated by a major company rivalling the North Eastern. The Midland Railway also ran along the edge of the Dales and in 1865 opened a 5½-mile branch from Apperley junction, in the Aire Valley midway between Leeds and Bradford. It climbed through Guiseley to join the line up Wharfedale, but for once the North Eastern and Midland departed from their stance of mutual hostility and the six-mile Otley to Ilkley section was a joint venture.

The Midland Railway had been formed in 1844 by a merger of existing companies and had a main line handling traffic from London into Leeds. It was an expansionist concern and an obvious route for growth was provided by the Aire Valley, then also commonly known as Airedale. It offered the lowest

5MT No.45446 approaches Settle junction with a Heysham to Leeds train in June 1960.
It is on the 'little' North Western Railway completed in 1850, with the Settle–Carlisle
railway on the right immediately beginning its almost unbroken 15-mile climb at 1 in 100
up Ribblesdale. The flat-topped peak of Ingleborough is on the far left. Derek Cross

of all possible crossings of the Pennines scarcely exceeding the 500ft contour,
which had earlier been followed by the Leeds & Liverpool Canal completed in
1819. A first stage saw incorporation in 1844 of the Leeds & Bradford Railway,
linking the two cities by an indirect route through the valley in order to secure
easy gradients. In 1846 it was leased to the Midland Railway on what were seen
as highly dubious terms. George Hudson was chairman of both companies and
these events were to play a pivotal role in his subsequent downfall.

Opening from Leeds to Bradford took place in July 1846 followed by
a series of extensions from Shipley through to Keighley, then Skipton and
finally in 1848 to Colne, where an end-on junction was made with lines in
Lancashire. The railway added to the growth of textile mills and urban sprawl
started by the canal. Dr E.W. Benson, Archbishop of Canterbury, was later to
lament on a visit to Keighley: 'The whole valley from end to end is spoiled,
enslaved, dejected. It was the very home and spring of fresh air and water, and
now it is a sewer of smoke, with a mantling ditch'. Understandably the former
name of 'Airedale', with its connotations of especially attractive scenery, largely
gave way to 'Aire Valley'.

Development of a railway on a route already taken by a canal was relatively

The Settle–Carlisle line – unquestionably the most spectacular railway in the Dales – was conceived as a link with Scotland rather than to serve this corner of Yorkshire. Class 40 No.D200 is entering the Dales as it crosses Lunds viaduct with an up special on 28 April 1984. Immediately to the north is the line's 1,169ft summit at Ais Gill, with the heights of Wild Boar Fell at top left. Gavin Morrison

straightforward, but the next move by the Midland was going to be a more complex affair. There was a clear need for a line linking the West Riding with Scotland. Out of many schemes during the Mania period there emerged the North Western Railway, incorporated in 1846 to build a main line extending from Skipton and running alongside the southern and western edges of the Dales for most of its length. Passing close to Settle, a branch to Lancaster would diverge at Clapham. Its main line would then continue through Ingleton to serve Kirkby Lonsdale and Sedbergh before a junction at Low Gill, 4½ miles south of Tebay, with the Lancaster & Carlisle Railway. This company formed a key component of the West Coast main line and from its opening in December 1846 was worked by the London & North Western Railway – soon commonly known as the 'Premier Line'.

In contrast its potential neighbour gained the less impressive nickname of the 'little' North Western to avoid confusion between the two concerns. It proved small in terms of capital resources and the difficult years following the

Redmire, an intermediate station on the single line through Wensleydale which took 30 years to complete from Northallerton to Hawes Junction. It now forms the western terminus of the preserved Wensleydale Railway, which is able to handle charter specials from the main-line network as seen here on 18 February 1990. Visible above the front of the HST is Bolton Castle. Gavin Morrison

Mania period forced a total change in strategy. The Clapham to Low Gill section involved heavy engineering and it was decided it should be deferred in favour of completing a link with Lancaster. A connection could be made here with the West Coast main line, and although it would now provide a less direct route to the north it would be much cheaper to build.

Construction between Clapham and Ingleton was so far advanced that it was decided to complete this section as far as what was seen as a temporary terminus, with a service over the 25 miles from Skipton beginning in July 1849. Those leaving the train at Ingleton can scarcely have failed to notice the partially constructed viaduct spanning the river Greta but would have no inkling that it was destined to remain in this state for another twelve years.

What had become the main line to Lancaster opened in June 1850 and there were now rail links to London and Scotland for both Skipton and Settle, two important gateway towns to the Dales. The Midland purchased the Leeds & Bradford Railway in 1851 and the following year arranged to work the 'little'

North Western, but the indirect route northwards involving a change of trains at Lancaster was far from ideal. There matters stood until an improvement in money supply led in 1857 to both the Lancaster & Carlisle and the 'little' North Western promoting rival schemes for the missing link from Ingleton to Low Gill. Parliament preferred the former and Yorkshire folk no doubt looked forward to much easier journeys to Scotland.

Unfortunately they were to be frustrated by the divisive railway politics of the mid-nineteenth century. In 1859 the Midland leased the 'little' North Western but was becoming at odds with the 'Premier Line', which in turn leased the Lancaster & Carlisle. Ingleton was now destined to be a railway frontier between two major and increasingly hostile companies. There was little incentive to complete the 22-mile Ingleton to Low Gill link but it was finally opened as an unimportant branch line in September 1861. Although they may be slightly exaggerated, many pen pictures have been painted of passengers having to leave their Midland train at Ingleton. Their voluminous Victorian luggage was then conveyed through the village to the north end of the viaduct, where the 'Premier Line' had its own station, and they would arrive just in time to see the so-called 'connection' disappearing into the distance.

By a quirk of boundaries a two-mile stretch of the Low Gill line either side of Sedbergh was the first railway in what today is the Yorkshire Dales National Park. There is a strong argument that there should have been no others. Just as the wild and sparsely populated centre of the Dales should have deterred railways from venturing further up Wensleydale or Wharfedale, so what was potentially a through line from Leeds to Carlisle via Ingleton and Low Gill was logically the best, most direct and relatively low-lying route from the West Riding to Scotland. Yet two of the largest and most powerful railway companies in Britain – the Midland and the London & North Western – refused to see it that way. Their constant rivalry and sheer obstinacy was to cast reasoning to one side and bring railways in the Dales from the periphery to the heartland. The ordinary became the improbable.

Main line through the mountains

THE Midland soon made it clear that it was not content with the state of affairs at Ingleton and threatened to build its own railway to Carlisle. There was only one possible route through the Dales, leaving the Skipton–Lancaster line to the south of Settle. It would climb continuously to a great viaduct at the head of Ribblesdale and then run above the 1,000ft contour for fifteen miles, audaciously tunnelling into the flanks of Dentdale and then Garsdale to reach one of the great watersheds of northern England where the rivers Ure and Eden rise within yards of one another. It would then crest a summit at Ais Gill before beginning a long descent to Carlisle through the Eden Valley. With no sharp curves or gradients steeper than 1 in 100, it would be the world's only railway built for express running through such mountainous terrain.

It was an extraordinarily ambitious and expensive concept but there was again a rash of cheap money supply and in 1866 the Midland obtained parliamentary sanction to proceed. No sooner had this occurred than the Overend Gurney banking failure sparked a financial crisis. Midland shareholders, already faced with the costs of completing their grandiose St Pancras terminus, took fright at the line's estimated cost of £2.4 million [2016 = £200 million]. It was decided to abandon thoughts of independent access to Carlisle and instead patch up a working agreement to use the London & North Western from Ingleton northwards. Some would see such a move as common-sense, as for over half its distance the proposed route from Settle to Carlisle was no more than ten miles from the parallel West Coast main line.

At this stage there was one fundamental snag. Abandonment of an authorised railway also needed parliamentary approval and this was vehemently opposed by other companies at odds with the 'Premier Line' and desperate to see a third Anglo-Scottish route. Parliament insisted in 1869 on the Settle–Carlisle line going ahead, a situation that would have led many lesser concerns into shoddy construction to the lowest possible standards. Not so the Midland, never a company to pursue matters in a half-hearted fashion and with its proud reputation to uphold. Instead of cheeseparing, it built one of the finest and most spectacular railways in Britain to express standards in a way that was nothing short of magnificent. John Sidney Crossley, the company's chief engineer, agreed to postpone retirement to see the line through to completion. It was perhaps inevitable that it went as much as 50 per cent over budget at a total cost of £3.6 million [2016 = £305 million], a colossal sum that meant there was no official ceremony when opening finally took place in May 1876. Conceived out of frustration and completed in desperation, it is unlikely the railway has ever repaid its capital cost, either directly or indirectly.

The Settle–Carlisle was primarily a main line to Scotland and scarcely served the Dales. In truth there was little to serve. Settle now had a station in the centre of the town more convenient than that on the Skipton-Lancaster line, now renamed Giggleswick, but it was not considered worth stopping express trains. Further north, the few local services called at Horton-in-Ribblesdale but then the landscape got truly wild and when the line first opened the next station was 24 miles distant at Kirkby Stephen in the Eden Valley. The railway passing through this mountain wilderness was the equivalent of a Roman road heading straight as an arrow to a distant destination with scant regard for anything on its way.

15

Developments in Wensleydale

WITH its sights set so firmly on Scotland, it might seem odd that the Midland should bother to build a six-mile branch to serve the small market town of Hawes close to the head of Wensleydale. It was in fact another example of the robust railway politics of the age and a product of mutual suspicion. Wensleydale provided one of the few east-west routes across the northern Pennines and the Midland saw a branch to Hawes as preventing any bid by the North Eastern to extend westwards. For its part, the ever-watchful North Eastern was nervous that the Midland would seize the opportunity to penetrate deep into its territory. It offered to subscribe half the cost towards a railway authorised in 1865 to link Ripon with Hawes. Diverging from the Leeds–Thirsk line at Melmerby, it would pass close to Masham before a junction at Finghall with the Leyburn branch which would then be continued westwards up the dale.

Economic reality now intervened in the same way as it had threatened the Settle–Carlisle. The independent Melmerby to Hawes line was abandoned and the North Eastern decided on a different strategy to 'block' any aspirations by the Midland. In 1870 it obtained powers for its own 16½-mile extension from Leyburn to Hawes and the following year was persuaded to go ahead with a branch from Melmerby as far as Masham.

Rather in the manner of a land grab, the two rival companies had now secured their territorial claims and actual construction took second place. With its length of only 7¾ miles the Masham branch was the first to be completed. It opened in June 1875, although its drawback was always that it was distant from the town on the opposite side of the river Ure.

The extension from Leyburn finally reached the small village of Askrigg in February 1877 and there was perhaps little surprise that further progress was delayed by disagreements over a joint station at Hawes. Not until June 1878 did it begin to be used by North Eastern services from Northallerton, which were introduced without any advance publicity. By October they were continuing over the Midland branch to remote Hawes Junction (later renamed Garsdale) on the Settle–Carlisle line.

Opposite, top: Opened as late as 1902, the Yorkshire Dales Railway linking Skipton with Grassington was all that came to pass of ambitious schemes for a direct main line from Manchester to Newcastle. In the summer of 1968 it achieved belated fame by becoming the last steam-worked branch line on British Railways, epitomised by Class 4 No.75019 trundling up to Swinden Quarry with ballast empties. David Rodgers

Lower: Heavy trains from Swinden Quarry have continued to be a welcome sight, greatly reducing lorry traffic on local roads. The Tilcon train for Hull is winding through classic Dales scenery near Rylstone on 1 May 1995 headed by Class 60 No.60027. Gavin Morrison

There was at last a link between two Anglo-Scottish main lines, although it was never to become more than a largely single-track cross-country byway. A welcome development occurred at the east end of the line, where services had to suffer the inconvenience of reversing out of Northallerton station until a direct curve was brought into use in September 1882.

The missing link

THE Dales came remarkably close to getting a second main line through its heartland. Seen as a necessity during the Mania years was a direct link between Manchester and Newcastle, two of the greatest cities in northern England. A straight line drawn on a map passed close to Grasington and Leyburn and various schemes were soon mooted.

Successfully incorporated in June 1846 was the Liverpool, Manchester & Newcastle-upon-Tyne Junction Railway, its grandiose title reflecting cities that would provide finance rather than proposed new lines. Actual construction would be a far shorter affair, with scarcely 50 miles separating the authorised Skipton to Colne line and the Richmond branch. Connecting the two would be relatively straightforward, as the Ice Age had created a U-shaped glacial valley that would provide a straight and easily-graded route through Upper Wharfedale. Similar conditions applied in continuing down Bishopdale towards Leyburn and Richmond. A two-mile tunnel would be required between the heads of the two dales but this was shorter than the three-mile bore already completed at Woodhead on the Manchester to Sheffield line. The summit would be only some 750ft above sea level in a sheltered valley bottom and construction would surely have been much easier than the challenges later faced on the windswept heights traversed by the Settle–Carlisle.

A line through the heart of the Dales was just one more symbol of glorious economic progress in the dawn of the Victorian age. The growth of trade was paramount and giving priority to protection of the countryside was still an alien concept that belonged to the future. A wave of confidence saw much of the route staked out, but then came collapse of the Railway Mania and further work was abandoned. So vanished a line that would have shortened the journey between Manchester and Newcastle to some 130 miles compared with the present-day 148 miles via Leeds and York.

Various attempts at revival failed on economic grounds and it was only in 1880 that amenity issues came to the fore. Igniting a wave of protest was the proposed crossing of the river Ure at the justifiably famous Aysgarth Falls. An outcry led to the formation of the Aysgarth Defence Association, supported by John Ruskin, which arranged public meetings and published a book attacking 'the railway vandal'. Sensing a rising tide of anger, it was arranged that Turner's

The Nidd Valley Light Railway from Pateley Bridge to Lofthouse formed an integral part of Bradford Corporation's construction of two massive reservoirs at the head of Nidderdale. Opening ceremonies at Lofthouse station on 11 September 1907 were on a grand scale. Author's collection

famous painting of the Falls should be exhibited in London so that those in the capital were aware of the beauty that was in danger of being destroyed.

The tirade reached a peak in 1884 and soon afterwards the railway promoters went into retreat. It was arguably the last realistic chance of such a line being built through the heart of the Dales. It would have totally transformed Upper Wharfedale and Bishopdale and the boundaries of today's National Park could have been very different. Unspoilt countryside now gives delight to both residents and visitors, and surely even the most way-out of think tanks would not have the temerity to suggest HS4 as a direct link between Manchester and Newcastle.

Last lines

ONLY three more railways were constructed in the Dales, none of them of great length. Despite the furore over Aysgarth Falls, there was little opposition when the Midland decided to build an 11½-mile link line from Ilkley to Skipton. It would also serve the scenic jewel of Bolton Abbey, already made famous by Wordsworth and Turner as well as Ruskin. Parliament paid little regard to aesthetic considerations and the only issue was the familiar one of placating a major landowner, in this case the 7th Duke of Devonshire who had one of his country seats at Bolton Abbey. He insisted that embankments and cuttings through his estate should be neatly covered with sods of turf and that no trees liable to interfere with signals should be felled without his consent. The line was duly opened as far as Bolton Abbey in May 1888 and five months later was extended through Embsay to Skipton.

It provided the springboard for a nine-mile branch from Embsay Junction to Grassington. The major railway companies might by now be showing little further interest in the area but this was not the case among local worthies. Their efforts led to incorporation in 1897 of the Yorkshire Dales Railway, opened in July 1902 and from the outset worked by the Midland. As at Masham, a fundamental problem was that the terminus was on the opposite side of the river to the sizeable village it purported to serve. In this case it had been sighted in the optimistic hope that it might still be possible to justify the company's title and continue northwards to Wensleydale. Realistically, it was now too late in the day to finance a line that would run through the middle of nowhere and involve construction of a two-mile tunnel.

Envious eyes must have been cast over the hill a few miles to the east where one of the finest light railways in Britain was built with little regard to cost. It was the creation of the city of Bradford, then the undoubted wool capital of the world and desperately needing to augment water supplies to its many mills. An immense project included building reservoirs at the head of Nidderdale in a desolate waste at the foot of Great and Little Whernside. A more remote location in the Dales would be difficult to conceive and it was clear that materials could only be brought to the site by rail. A contractor's line was built over the six miles from the nearest road at Lofthouse but a completely new railway was needed to reach this point from the existing North Eastern branch terminus at Pateley Bridge.

The Board of Trade agreed to it being built under the provisions of the 1896 Light Railways Act providing a public passenger service was also operated. Many dubious and ramshackle undertakings took advantage of the lesser standards permitted under the Act, but this was not the approach adopted by Bradford in its high noon of prosperity. The six-mile Nidd Valley Light Railway – the only such venture ever to be operated by a municipality – was blessed with full signalling and stone-built stations when it opened in September 1907.

Declining years

THE Nidd Valley Light Railway had a brief life of only 23 years. Construction of a first reservoir at Angram was finished in 1917 and work at neighbouring Scar House had peaked by the late 1920s. Motor bus and lorry competition was becoming serious and Bradford Corporation withdrew public passenger and goods services in January 1930. Road competition similarly affected the

Grassington and Masham branches, both of which were now vulnerable to an inconvenient terminus some distance from the communities they had been built to serve. Grassington lost its passenger services in September 1930 and Masham in January 1931.

There matters rested until after the Second World War when the first casualty was the Pateley Bridge branch, losing its passenger services in April 1951 and seeing a gradual decline in goods workings until these ended thirteen years later. More strenuous opposition greeted a proposal to withdraw trains between Northallerton and Hawes but it proved unsuccessful and it was a sad day in Wensleydale when they ended in April 1954. Hawes station itself remained open for a token service of one train a day from Garsdale until March 1959 when this section of line was completely closed. Goods traffic west of Redmire ceased in April 1964.

It was not therefore the Beeching Report that played havoc with railways in the Dales. Economic reality had already done its worst and, apart from main lines skirting the area, all that remained in passenger terms were the Settle–Carlisle; the secondary routes from Leeds to Skipton through Ilkley via Guiseley and Otley now worked by diesel multiple units; and the Richmond branch. There was little left to be pruned but March 1965 saw passenger services cease from Leeds via Otley to Ilkley as well as further west through Bolton Abbey to Skipton. An especially effective local campaign saved the line into Ilkley through Guiseley and it survived to be transformed by electrification in 1995. Opposition to closure of the Richmond branch was not so successful and after a brave fight its passenger traffic ended in March 1969 with freight ceasing eleven months later.

Two lines on the fringe of the Dales were also casualties. The link from Clapham through Ingleton to Low Gill lost its local trains in February 1954, but three of its stations were close to schools catering for boarders. Beginning and end-of-term specials continued to call at Kirkby Lonsdale (for Cressbrook and the town's grammar school), Barbon (for Casterton) and Sedbergh (for the public school of the same name). The route was also used for diversionary purposes, especially in the winter of 1963 when the Settle–Carlisle was blocked by snow. Retaining the line for such occasional traffic was eventually deemed a luxury and complete closure took place in July 1966.

Far more serious was the closure a year later of the main line north from Harrogate which had once had junctions for both Pateley Bridge and Masham. Its express services from Leeds to Newcastle and Scotland were diverted via York leaving Ripon as a cathedral city with no railway. Thus by the dawn of the 1970s the only railways left in the Dales were the Settle–Carlisle and the Ilkley line through Guiseley with quarry traffic still using the

The first preservation venture in the Dales came to fruition at Embsay station
in May 1979 using industrial locomotives such as this Hunslet 0-6-0ST.
The line was extended to Bolton Abbey in May 1998. Embsay Steam Railway

Grassington branch as far as Swinden and also working up Wensleydale from
Northallerton to Redmire.

Even the Settle–Carlisle was no longer secure. Way back in 1923 its heyday
was over when the Midland became part of the LMS and it was now of
secondary importance. Gradually it became an ever-more-expensive duplicate
route, virtually neglected by photographers who in the steam age favoured the
more epic locations of Shap and Beattock. Fears that it would be abandoned in
favour of the shorter route through Ingleton proved groundless, but by the
1960s maintenance was being cut to a minimum, speed restrictions enforced
and the whole line began to take on an air of neglect. A yo-yo of policy changes
saw withdrawal of local services in 1970 followed only five years later by the
reopening of closed stations for Dales Rail charter trains. In 1981 began the infamous closure proposal centred round the alleged critical condition of
Ribblehead viaduct. It attracted unprecedented opposition, only ending in
1989 when Michael Portillo, then the Transport Minister, announced that the
Secretary of State was refusing consent.

It took seven long years for the Midland to build the Settle–Carlisle and
British Rail a year longer in its attempts to achieve closure. For the second time
in the line's history, a railway company was now compelled to spend reluctant

Leeming Bar became the eastern terminus of the preserved Wensleydale Railway when the line was reopened as far as Leyburn in July 2003. In earlier times, J21 0-6-0 No.65075 is pausing alongside the characteristic North Eastern 'split-post' signal with a short milk train. The buildings on the right typified the stations by G.T. Andrews criticised for 'wanton extravagance'. Author's collection

millions. To its credit, BR followed the stance adopted by its predecessor and metaphorically rolled up its sleeves to get on with the job. Symbolic of the transformation were day-and-night repairs to Ribblehead viaduct in October 1989 with floodlighting forming a weird spectacle in such desolate surroundings.

Preservation

THE Settle–Carlisle saga has tended to divert attention from two preservation ventures that have played an important role in fostering Dales tourism. When the Ilkley to Skipton line closed for through traffic in 1965 it still remained in use at its western end, primarily because it was handling mineral trains from Swinden Quarry on the extant portion of the Grassington branch. It was also serving Hawbank Quarry, immediately east of Embsay station, which continued to dispatch ballast until October 1968.

Track lifting at Embsay should then have been the next step but was destined never to take place. Instead the station played a pivotal role in the formation of a preservation society with the initial object of establishing a working transport museum. It adopted the same name of the Yorkshire Dales Railway as used by the promoters of the Grassington branch and it also had gestation problems. Not until May 1979 did the granting of a Light Railway Order permit opening of a short stretch of line heading west from the station to Bow Bridge. Priority was then given to extending in stages in the opposite direction with an obvious goal being Bolton Abbey, now a tourist honeypot. This was realised in May 1998 when what was now the 3½-mile Embsay & Bolton Abbey Steam Railway was formally opened by Sir William McAlpine.

The ultimate goal has still not been achieved, as the hope remains that a connection might be made with the surviving Swinden Quarry line and thus run into Skipton. The quarry continues to dispatch long and heavy trains which have done much to reduce lorry traffic on local roads, but its life is not infinite and one day there will be a redundant branch that for much of its length is in a scenically superb setting. Linking it to the present steam railway is bound to be a dream prospect.

A very different story with quarry traffic led to a second preservation venture in the Dales. In December 1992 British Steel ceased using the Wensleydale branch for supplies of limestone from Redmire. A company was then formed to try and buy the line with a view to restoring passenger services but total closure seemed inevitable when British Rail quoted a price of £1 million. A fairy godmother then appeared on the scene in the unlikely form of the Ministry of Defence, increasingly concerned with problems in moving tanks between Salisbury Plain and Catterick Camp by road. It looked at the alternative of rail transport and the Wensleydale branch, with its Redmire terminus within a few miles of Catterick Garrison, was an obvious final link in any such arrangement.

Not only did the Ministry of Defence decide in 1995 to go ahead with this scheme but it also raised no objections to the Wensleydale Railway Company taking over the branch and agreed to finance essential improvements. As at Embsay, there were procedural delays but in July 2003 a passenger service over the 11¾ miles between Leeming Bar and Leyburn was inaugurated by William Hague, the local MP. It was an impressive ceremony including a flypast by RAF Leeming and the ringing of bells at 14 churches within sound of the railway. A year later services were extended over an additional 4½ miles to Redmire. Again there are similarities with Embsay in that an ultimate goal is restoring a direct main-line connection, in this case with the East Coast route at Northallerton. A temporary platform a mile distant from the main station was provided at Northallerton West in November 2014, but at times it must all seem an impossibly long haul. Yet it has to be remembered that completion of the line as far as Redmire took no less than 31 years so arguably the local community must continue to be patient.

Chapter Two

Wharfedale

Rails to Ilkley

ILKLEY was merely a village with less than 800 inhabitants when railway promotion reached fever pitch in 1846. It nevertheless stood little chance of escaping the hysteria of the Railway Mania as it occupied a strategic position in Lower Wharfedale. A new era seemed about to dawn with the flotation of the cumbersomely named Lancashire & Yorkshire North Eastern Railway – starting from the Aire valley in Skipton before crossing over into Wharfedale to reach Wetherby and then York. It is unlikely that tiny Ilkley would be a major consideration in the eyes of its promoters, but this would not be the case with the neighbouring town of Otley which was then over four times its size. The proposed line started railway rivalry between the two centres that was to continue for the next 150 years and ultimately result in what was originally much the larger settlement being the loser.

Neither was to succeed in this first round. Hostility from the embryo Leeds & Thirsk Railway led to the scheme being abandoned east of Arthington, although at least the company was incorporated in July 1846 as the Wharfdale Railway (using the antiquated spelling for the valley). Local hopes must have started to run high, but the line was one of countless casualties of the collapse of the Mania period. It was left to private operators to run 'good, safe and convenient omnibuses from Ilkley and Otley to connect with trains at Arthington'.

As a market town, Otley predictably continued its long-established role of supplying agricultural produce to the urban areas centred on Leeds and Bradford. Ilkley might also have stayed little changed but was transformed by a Victorian fad. It was the obsession with retreating to a spa to take the waters. The now world-famous Ilkley Moor had long been noted for a spring at White Wells. As early as 1709, a Dr Richardson penned some distinctly barbed comments: 'Ilkley is now a very mean place, and equally dirty and insignificant, and chiefly famous for a cold well, which has done very remarkable cures in

Otley station, opened in February 1865. Its site is now a bypass and the town
is bereft of rail facilities, whereas the once smaller Ilkley has a half-hourly service
to both Leeds and Bradford. L&GRP

scrofulous cases by bathing, and in drinking of it'. When railways were on the
horizon in the 1830s the waters were claimed to be excellent for those suffering
from 'long confinement in populous towns, effects arising from late hours, the
abuse of liquors &etc'. Their alleged properties were sufficient to impress
Charles Darwin, when he sought a cure for a mysterious ailment coinciding
with the publication of his controversial *On the Origin of Species*.

Darwin took hydropathic treatment at the massive Wells House built in
1856. It had been preceded twelve years earlier by the even grander Ben
Rhydding Hydro, a mile to the east, complete with baths of every description,
a bowling green, croquet lawns and a racket court, all 'adapted to drive away
dull care'. Ilkley clearly stood on the brink of a new age of grand living and all
it needed was a railway to bring the great and the good to a spa soon to be
known as 'the Malvern of the North'.

Various abortive schemes finally led local interests to approach both the
Midland and the North Eastern in 1859. When these normally warring
companies both sensed that great opportunities might lie round the corner and
for once agreed to sink their differences, they adopted what the noted writer
Ernest Leopold Ahrons succinctly termed 'a hostile courtesy'. Progress with
the resulting Otley & Ilkley Joint Railway was nevertheless slow.

On the North Eastern connection from Arthington to Otley, there
were problems with the gentry in the shape of the redoubtable Francis

Completion of the line to Skipton in 1888 made Ilkley a popular destination for
excursion traffic from Lancashire and Cheshire. 'Patriot' 4-6-0 No.45505 *The Royal
Army Ordnance Corps* is heading back to Whaley Bridge, near Stockport, with a
half-day working on 15 May 1955. Both the overbridge and Woolworth's store
on its right have ceased to be features of the town. F.W. Smith

Hawkesworth Fawkes whose forebears had graced Farnley Hall for two
centuries. Noted for having 'a singularly red bird-like eye and the keen vision
of a born gunner', he often hosted his close friend and England's greatest
landscape painter, Joseph Mallord William Turner. This may explain why he
was so implacably opposed to a railway disfiguring the landscape, although his
protests and pamphleteering proved out of step with the times and achieved
little. After agreement was reached to put a stretch of line in a cutting,
construction went ahead in the spring of 1863 in time for trains to reach Otley
in February 1865.

It was landslips that delayed opening of the Midland connection from
Apperley junction and the joint line into Ilkley until August 1865. At the
terminus there was what was considered suitable segregation by means of
separate 1st class waiting rooms for gentlemen and ladies, who unlike the men
also had their own 2nd class facilities. An early development occurred when
Ben Rhydding Hydro paid for the building of 'a small wooden station'
complete with 'retiring room for ladies', where its clients were met by horse-
bus. It was opened in July 1866 and replaced five years later by a more
permanent stone structure, which in 1885 ceased to be a private station and
was sold to the Joint Railway for £240 [2016 = £23,500].

Arrangements on the Otley & Ilkley Joint generally seemed to work better than was often the case with such lines, although Ahrons noted the problems that could arise if a passenger using a season ticket issued by one company attempted to enter a train operated by the other. He recalled: 'One martinet of a local stationmaster was so rabid on this subject, and exercised so much Prussian discipline over the travelling public, that the latter turned, like the proverbial worm, and retaliated by invariably and purposely getting into the opposite company's trains, from which they refused to be ejected'. It took several months for peace to be restored.

Further up the dale

THE coming of railways to Lower Wharfedale immediately affected the population figures. Otley had fractionally declined from 4,751 in 1851 to 4,714 ten years later, but now there was a sudden increase in the 1871 census to 5,855. Enabled to make the most of its spa status, the change at Ilkley was even more dramatic. The number of inhabitants more than doubled from 1,043 in 1861 to 2,511 in 1871 and almost doubled again to reach 4,736 in 1881.

Visitors came in ever increasing numbers and many of them now wanted to go further. Those who considered themselves the upper classes would often club together to travel by reserved saloon to Ilkley and then by wagonettes to Bolton Abbey. Proposals to make this scenic jewel more accessible inevitably divided opinion. Fred Cobley, writing On Foot through Wharfedale in 1882, summed up the arguments and pointed a finger at the red rose county:

> The iron horse has not yet penetrated this delightful portion of the valley. How long this will hold true, however, I cannot state, for a movement is now on foot having for its object the construction of a railway which will connect Ilkley with Skipton, and so open out to the dwellers in Lancashire a more direct route to these parts. While such an innovation will by some be regarded as fatal to the peacefulness which now adds beauty to the scene, others will welcome it as a boon, very much needed and long ago expected.

When need triumphed over peace and the Midland completed the line in 1888 there was indeed a sudden change at Bolton Abbey. The station immediately became a highly popular destination, despite being well over a mile distant from the ruins of the famous priory. The contemporary historian Harry Speight descended from the moral high ground to recognise that the railway meant 'even the lowliest denizens of such smoke-palled cities as Leeds and Bradford may for a comparatively trifling outlay enjoy communion with some

An image that might appear to be the main-line platforms at Skipton station.
It is in fact the Ilkley platforms in their full Midland glory as opened in 1888 with
canopies that did not survive LMS days. They were at a slightly higher level to minimise
the gradient for eastbound trains but the start could still prove challenging. L&GRP

of the noblest achievements of man'. On completion of the line through to
Skipton in October 1888 they could be joined by those suffering life in the
equally begrimed Lancashire cotton towns.

Services far and wide

CHANGES were now afoot in Ilkley. It was again Fred Cobley who in 1882
noted with true Victorian verbosity that its 'excellently-constructed streets,
its tastefully designed villas and its extensive hydropathic establishments,
boarding houses and hotels are all more or less impressed with the stamp of
newness'. Adopting a strange figure of speech, he couldn't resist adding:
'Hotels, some of them very grand and commodious, stand as thick as
blackberries. At each the visitor will receive the best of everything.'

The Victorian fad for hydropathy was by now on the wane. Yet it left behind
a settlement perfectly suited as a dormitory town for the wealthy middle
classes of Bradford and Leeds, who did not want to be too close to the hell
holes that many of them had created. It was especially popular with the wool
merchants of Bradford, who by 1888 enjoyed a service of twelve trains each

A typical three-carriage train from Leeds to Ilkley via Otley approaches Ben Rhydding behind an ex-North Eastern G5 0-4-4T, circa 1950. These services were withdrawn in March 1965. G.T.G. Findlay

way daily. The fastest was conveniently timed to leave at 8.30am and complete the journey in just half an hour, two minutes faster than today's electric services.

These pioneer commuters had the benefit of competition when travelling to Leeds. A Midland train pulled out of Ilkley at 8.10am and reached Leeds Wellington at 9am but five minutes later there was a North Eastern service running non-stop beyond Otley and arriving at Leeds New at 8.52am. Collectively the Midland and North Eastern provided seventeen trains each way daily between Ilkley and Leeds. In the opposite direction, services beyond Ilkley to Skipton were considerably more modest with five trains each way.

Through workings to or from points further afield gradually made their appearance with a Midland summer service between Manchester and Ilkley being introduced in 1890. From about 1900 there was a daily through carriage to London, leaving Ilkley at 1.15pm and being attached to a King's Cross train at Leeds to reach the capital at 6.10pm. A more startling innovation in 1908 was a summer Saturday St Pancras to Edinburgh express complete with restaurant car in those civilised days before pre-packed food. Omitting a stop at Leeds, it called at Ilkley and was then in Carlisle in a little over two hours – a journey time that is no longer remotely possible. The North Eastern was equally enterprising in the summer of 1913 when it put on through carriages from Harrogate to Heysham in connection with the Isle of Man steamers. The outbreak of the First World War caused all these ventures to be terminated.

At various times the North Eastern operated services from York or Harrogate to Bolton Abbey or Skipton using autocars – its name for a push-and-pull unit often with the engine sandwiched between two coaches. The LNER similarly used Sentinel steam railcars between York and Bolton Abbey, which had become a popular destination for excursion trains from Lancashire and the North East. Their arrival no doubt kept the station staff busy, although it was nothing to compare with the high alert that arose on frequent occasions when a double-headed royal train brought King George V to stay with the Duke of Devonshire at Bolton Hall.

As the country came out of recession in the late 1930s, there was a re-run of past events with the introduction of through services that were to be abruptly terminated by war. They included a Leeds–Morecambe train via Ilkley, but all such enterprise came to an abrupt end with imposition of an emergency timetable in September 1939. Economy measures included closure of Bolton Abbey station from June 1940 to March 1941. A very different kind of traffic was to raise the echoes through Otley and Ilkley. Heavy coal and coke trains came this way *en route* from the Newport-on-Tees area to Barrow-in-Furness and down the Colne line to Lancashire. Double-headed and by 1943 often amounting to eight trains in each direction, they made a spectacular sight and sound and frequently took more than an hour to get from Ilkley to Skipton.

Changing times

THE pre-war variety of services was never regained, but a summer Saturday working from Saltburn to Blackpool via Harrogate and Ilkley was introduced in 1946 and survived until 1963. The locomotive taking it through to Colne came back on the return train and often had trouble in re-starting on the curved 1 in 85 straight off the platform edge at Skipton. A banker was kept in readiness in the days when it was loading to ten or more carriages. Challenging workings in the opposite direction were tanker trains from Billingham to Heysham, which by 1954 were so heavy that they were often double-headed.

Diesel multiple units made their debut in 1957 with summer Sunday trains from Castleford via Leeds Central and Otley to Bolton Abbey. They preceded dieselisation of virtually all Lower Wharfedale services on 5 January 1959, a date that saw simultaneous closure of the two-road engine shed at Ilkley. Trains from Ilkley through Guiseley to both Leeds and Bradford were now almost twice as frequent with improved journey times. By contrast Otley received a cold shoulder with services limited to four each way reduced to three in 1960. It was the beginning of the end and may explain why the town made little effective protest when the 1963 Beeching Report recommended closure of all railways serving Lower Wharfedale. Commuters using the improved services from Ilkley to Leeds and Bradford via Guiseley were much more vociferous. They formed the Ilkley Railway Supporters' Association, which played a key role in attracting over 2,500 written objections and led to the Minister of Transport deciding in September 1964 to defer a closure decision on this section of line.

The remaining railways were not so fortunate and the March 1965 withdrawal of all passenger services from Ilkley to Leeds via Otley, as well as Ilkley to Skipton, was soon followed by track-lifting operations. A humorous note among all the gloom was provided at Pool, east of Otley. Early one morning in May 1966 a local farmer found the demolition team had left a long line of wagons obstructing the crossing used by his milking herd. Quite what he had to say to Leeds Train Control is not recorded and was probably unprintable, but it resulted in the hasty dispatch of a rescue locomotive from Holbeck shed at the unearthly hour of 5.30am!

A new era

THERE can be few better instances of the utterly unexpected coming to pass than what has happened on the surviving line into Ilkley since the 1964 closure proposal. The deferral of any decision remained in place for no less than eight years with a consequent rundown in facilities. Finally in 1972 the Minister of Transport announced that the Leeds to Ilkley line had been reprieved. Formation of the West Yorkshire Passenger Transport Executive in April 1974 then brought improvements to the intermediate stations and the introduction in 1978 of an hourly interval service from Ilkley to both Leeds and Bradford. 'Pacer' units operating in smart red and cream West Yorkshire livery helped to double passenger numbers through the 1980s. Those who had campaigned in the mid-1960s can scarcely have dreamt of the ultimate outcome, which came in November 1990 when the Government approved plans for electrification.

The scheme was coupled with the Aire Valley lines from Leeds and Bradford to Skipton, but these had never been threatened in quite the same way. It was including Ilkley that caused the real surprise, as few railways have gone from likely closure to the benefits of electric traction in so short a time span. Work soon got under way on what overall was the largest electrification project in Britain since completion of that on the East Coast main line. Ilkley services were withdrawn for six weeks in the summer of 1992 to permit major upgrading.

The downside of it all was that shortage of rolling stock meant class 308 EMUs built as long ago as 1957 were all that was available to start electric services during 1995. It was not until 2001 that there came a vastly superior upgrade with today's class 333s, newly built in Zaragoza, Spain and brought to Leeds through the Channel Tunnel.

Commuters are now as well content as can ever be the case with rail users. They benefit from low fares and there is a train every half hour into the city centres of both Bradford and Leeds. By contrast those living in Otley have to use the bus or face a nightmare car journey followed by expensive parking fees. They must often reflect on what went wrong. If only a few miles of line had been retained and the station not sacrificed to a bypass, their life would have been very different.

Rails to Grassington

RAILWAY development in Upper Wharfedale had few similarities with the lower part of the valley. A line extending beyond Bolton Abbey to Grassington was never seriously contemplated as the market and service centre was always Skipton rather than Ilkley. Once all hope collapsed of a main line passing through Grassington as it linked Manchester with Newcastle, the efforts to build a far more modest branch from Skipton were initially led by Sir Mathew Wilson Bart of Eshton Hall, near Gargrave. When he died in 1891, he was succeeded by his son, who at the age of only sixteen confusingly became a second Sir Mathew Wilson Bart. Despite his young years, the then social order placed great store in the status of baronets and there was no doubt delight when he agreed to follow in his father's footsteps and back the new proposals.

His presence may well have helped to secure an easier passage for the company's incorporation in August 1897. Confidence was increased by the fact that the Midland had agreed to work the line and hand over 40 per cent of receipts. It was in this spirit of optimism that Sir Mathew found himself elected chairman of the Yorkshire Dales Railway at the age of twenty-two, but doubts soon arose as to whether he was the ideal man for the job. He failed to attend a meeting to finalise the prospectus and, more seriously, did not get to the formal cutting of the first sod in June 1900. By now he had already gained notoriety as a rake and ladies' man. His reputation was not helped when he threw a party at Eshton Hall for everyone from miles around whose surname included the word 'bottom'. He set his guests to work introducing themselves and then fled the scene!

It is perhaps no surprise that the financial affairs of the company soon drifted into chaos and it found itself unable to raise the required capital of £45,000 [2016 = £4 million]. It was only further support from the Midland that saved the day. In early 1902, Sir Mathew was replaced as chairman by Walter Morrison, who had undertaken the ceremonial sod cutting. Still remembered locally as a millionaire bachelor with his 'mountain home' at Malham Tarn, plain Mr Morrison had no airs and graces. He had made his fortune partly from manufacturing black crêpe, considered so essential at

Walter Morrison MP holding the silver spade, cuts the first sod of the Yorkshire Dales Railway at Grassington on 7 June 1900. Author's collection

The author's grandfather was a shareholder in the line and duly received an invitation to the ceremonial opening on 29 July 1902. It was a memorable occasion but he later regretted his investment! Author's collection

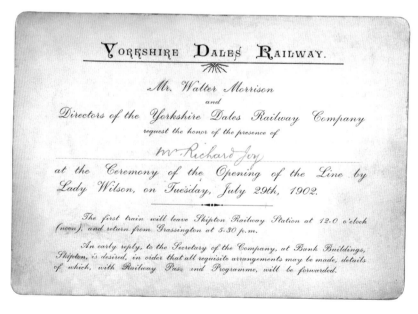

The line's terminus in about 1905, shortly after opening. Seats carrying the full name 'Grassington and Threshfield' are indicative that it stood midway between the two villages – a factor leading to withdrawal of passenger services as early as 1930.
Author's collection

Victorian funerals, but also from shrewd investments in Argentine railways. He thus had the required experience and, crucially at this critical time, was a director and later chairman of the Craven Bank, which numbered the Yorkshire Dales Railway among its customers. Letters from the bank about the company's parlous overdraft were now probably little more than a formality, as they were always answered with a 'suitable reply' that understandably was not questioned!

By the time of Walter Morrison's appointment the railway was well on its way to completion. Its construction must have seemed close to relaxation for the engineer Edgar Ferguson, who had previously acted in the same capacity on the portion of the Settle–Carlisle that included Ribblehead viaduct and Blea Moor tunnel. From Embsay junction on the Skipton–Ilkley line, the single-track branch climbed almost continuously at 1 in 75 for the first two miles as far as a siding for timber and stone traffic at Crookrise. Thereafter it was switchback, one of the few level portions being used for the only intermediate station at Rylstone. Like Grassington, it symbolised the straitened circumstances in being built of timber supplied by the aptly named Portable Buildings Company. The two structures respectively cost the modest amounts of £173 and £279 [2016 = £15,000 and £24,000].

Despite such economies, one of the few passenger-line openings of the Edwardian age in July 1902 was a memorable occasion. It was haymaking time and the organising committee regretted that it was 'short of full strength on account of several being busy on their farms'. Nevertheless, a village that had been waiting more than half a century since a railway connection was first mooted certainly did its best. A lengthy procession met the first train, resplendently decorated with flags and flowers, and a gargantuan formal lunch with speeches galore finished only just in time for the great and the good to catch the return special.

Normal services began with four trains daily each way with an additional working on Mondays and Saturdays. Grassington had greatly suffered from the collapse of lead mining, with its population sinking to its lowest-ever level of 480 in 1891, and the effect on the locality was immediate. Trains brought in crowds of holidaymakers and day visitors to see Upper Wharfedale, demanding meals, stimulating cafés and boarding houses and stirring up trade of all kinds.

One place the visitors did not get to see was the famous 260-acre Grass Woods, owned by leading local landowner the 8th Duke of Devonshire. He had been noticeably absent in lending support to the railway and in 1901 his agent, fearing 'the increased numbers of working-class visitors which the new line might bring', promptly declared the woods private. A long dispute began with keepers and estate servants being placed on guard at all entrances.

The railway also made commuting possible, leading to Grassington's population doubling within twenty years. A wave of new housing was epitomised by Bridge End, a red-roofed terrace overlooking the river. It quickly gained the colourful nickname of Boiled Egg Row, the theory being that dutiful wives saw the train arrive and could time an egg to be ready just as the husband crossed the threshold!

By 1906 there were six trains each way daily and four years later the growing number of commuters in the Bradford wool trade justified the provision of a radical new service. The 7.45am train from Grassington detached a through portion to Bradford at Embsay junction, from where it was taken on to Ilkley by a light engine. Here it was attached to a fast train to Bradford, due to arrive at 9am. In the opposite direction there was the novelty of a slip coach off the 5.10pm Morecambe residential, which became part of the 5.55pm departure from Skipton and reached Grassington at 6.23pm. Despite all the advances of the car age, the overall time of 1 hour 13 minutes cannot always be bettered in today's rush hour.

It was all too brief a heyday, although the continuing excursion traffic resumed after the war on the never-to-be forgotten Easter Monday of 1949. The first train from Bradford arrived with six hundred passengers crammed

Grassington continued to handle limestone traffic until about 1966. The stone was brought down from Skirethornes Quarry on a rope-worked narrow-gauge tramway and then tipped into standard-gauge wagons at this exchange siding. Author

into its coaches, but this proved to be modest compared with the following excursion from Leeds. It was estimated that around a thousand people had somehow got on board without any cases of suffocation, but progress up the long 1 in 75 from Embsay Junction severely winded the 4F 0-6-0 at its head. It pulled into Grassington over an hour late to be met by the district operating superintendent. His apologies went down badly, especially when it emerged that he had driven there by car.

Excursion traffic quickly recovered and through the 1950s many Bank Holidays saw four well-patronised trains descend on Grassington. They tailed away in the 1960s, by which time the line's terminus represented a true country railway displaying little sense of urgency. A goods train continued to bring in such essentials as coal, cattle food and even ice cream, although sometimes it would take an age to come up from Skipton. The inordinate delay was only explained when the driver produced a bag of mushrooms picked from fields bordering the line!

Minerals to the fore

WHEN Grassington station closed to goods traffic in 1969 it was still far from the end for most of the branch – and arguably the greatest single development was yet to come. It centred round the fact that the line passed alongside Swinden, one of a small group of geologically unique reef knolls formed in a similar way to the coral reefs of Australia. A scheme to quarry it was conceived the moment the Yorkshire Dales Railway was incorporated. P.W. Spencer, who owned limestone kilns in Lothersdale near Skipton, acquired rights at Swinden in 1899 and the branch opened with sidings in place to serve the first kiln. The *Railway Magazine* commented that it looked 'strangely out of place between the fields and the moorlands' and was to the detriment of the local scenery. A further five kilns, fed by an extensive network of narrow gauge tramways, had been constructed by 1914. It was the beginning of systematic quarrying that was to blight the immediate locality and destroy a rounded green hill but ultimately prove the saviour of most of the Grassington branch.

More intriguing were the schemes of John Delaney, whose enterprise in the area began when with great difficulty he raised £40 to buy a horse and cart to distribute coal from the newly opened Settle station. A tireless worker, he had by 1900 acquired more than a thousand private-owner wagons conveying coal over a wide part of Yorkshire. He also owned the limestone quarry at Horton-in-Ribblesdale served by the Settle–Carlisle railway. Soon after the branch reached Grassington he started to extract limestone at Skirethornes on the edge of Threshfield Moor, installing a 2ft 6in. gauge tramway worked by a steam-powered endless rope. This took the stone down to Delaney's Siding, opened at the terminus in 1904. There was no looking back and within fifteen years he had made an absolute fortune.

Traffic from this source had ceased by 1966 and it seemed only a matter of time before Swinden Quarry would go the same way. Then in 1970 its ownership passed to the newly formed Tilcon Ltd, which embarked on a massive expansion programme to double the output of limestone with siding capacity being greatly increased. The line up from Skipton received a complete upgrade to handle long and heavy trains that have continued to the present day and have done much to reduce lorry traffic on the local roads. There is a certain irony in that some of these trains have conveyed quarry products to the North East, travelling via York on an indirect route that the Yorkshire Dales Railway and its predecessors strove in vain to supersede.

Chapter Three

Ribblesdale, Dentdale and Garsdale

England's most spectacular railway

UNIQUE in running through three of the main valleys in the Dales, the Settle–Carlisle can largely be described in the present tense. It is the great survivor and stands alone among main-line railways in structurally remaining virtually as built.

It begins modestly enough in Ribblesdale, diverging at Settle junction from the earlier North Western line from Skipton to Ingleton and Lancaster. It then immediately begins an almost unbroken 15-mile climb at 1 in 100 to Blea Moor, nicknamed the 'Long Drag' by generations of perspiring enginemen. Within two miles is Settle station, its buildings in what might be termed standard 'Midland Gothic' notable for its ornate weatherboarding and massive proportions. The designer was the company's architect John Holloway Sanders, who was also responsible for the joint station of 1865 at Ilkley.

The railway is carried above Settle on two viaducts and a long embankment containing more than a million cubic yards of earth. The climb up Ribblesdale continues past Langcliffe and the Craven Quarry, which provided some of the first freight traffic on the line. Preserved as a remarkable underground labyrinth is its Hoffmann kiln, of German design, elliptical in shape to permit firing in a continuous circular movement. A short tunnel at Stainforth precedes Sheriff or Sherwood Brow, a limestone gorge that necessitated the construction of two skew viaducts and diversion of the river so that the railway could occupy its former course. Hereabouts the line shows how it has clearly become part of the surrounding landscape with its mixture of drystone walls and sweeping pastureland giving way to the crouching-lion shape of 2,273ft Penyghent, lowest but certainly not the least dramatic of the famous Three Peaks.

Quarries at Helwith Bridge and Horton-in-Ribblesdale were also early sources of mineral traffic with sidings respectively handling granite and limestone. Still climbing, the tracks pass the hamlet of Selside and then the strikingly positioned Salt Lake Cottages, built for railwaymen and like others on the route very much Midland in style. They make no attempt to harmonise with the local vernacular architecture.

Ribblehead station is surrounded by what a farmer once described as 'nowt but scenery' and in today's age of leisure is far busier with walkers than was ever the case when it handled purely local traffic. On the main building the end and projecting gables are tiled as an added protection against extreme weather conditions. These were recognised when in 1938 it became an official meteorological reporting point, with the stationmaster responsible for releasing hydrogen balloons in order to determine the height of cloud layers. It was perhaps unkindly said that he spent more time dispatching hourly weather reports than he did handling trains. Indicative of the lack of any nearby village is the fact that Sunday evensong was conducted in the waiting room by the vicar of Ingleton until as late as 1956.

Just beyond the station is the line's outstanding feature, the spectacular Ribblehead viaduct scheduled as both an Ancient Monument and a Grade II* listed structure. A quarter of a mile long and majestically curved, its 24 arches reach a maximum height of 104 feet above the boggy moorland. Its setting is magnificent and, despite its size, it is dwarfed by 2,373ft Ingleborough and 2,414ft Whernside, the two other Three Peaks of Yorkshire. The viaduct spans a notorious wind gap at the head of Chapel-le-Dale where westerly gales funnelling up from Morecambe Bay can exceed 100mph and in steam days often brought heavy trains to a halt.

From the wilds of Ribblehead, set amid its great amphitheatre of high mountains, the line curves gradually northwards to reach the railway outpost of Blea Moor. A place almost chilling in its remoteness and until recent times having no road access, electricity or running water, it was nevertheless from the outset a key location in traffic terms. Lie-by sidings and later passing loops were regularly used by heavy freight trains, frequently winded by the herculean climb up from Settle, which paused for breath and water while expresses dashed past on the main line. Here too was a cluster of cottages for permanent-way men and still in regular use is the signal-box, which must rank high among the most isolated in Britain.

The line next goes under Force Gill aqueduct carrying a beck over the railway and finally ends its long climb by entering the 1 mile 869yd Blea Moor tunnel, 500ft below ground level and predominantly on a downgrade of 1 in 440. Bored through rock of unrelieved hardness, it took five years to

The unmistakable setting of the Settle–Carlisle at Helwith Bridge with Penyghent dominant in the distance. Class 40 No.40094 is crossing the river Ribble with a down freight on 26 August 1981. Gavin Morrison

complete. Three permanent ventilation shafts gave rise to the nickname of 'Yorkshire's Smoky Mountain', although in certain atmospheric conditions the smoke from locomotives could be notoriously difficult to clear. A strange sight on Sundays when there were few trains must have been the local Methodist minister who pushed his bike over Ribblehead viaduct and then through the tunnel before pedalling off to preach at Dent chapel.

The northern exit from Blea Moor tunnel is one of the great dramatic moments of the Settle–Carlisle with the line running on a shelf high above green and winding Dentdale. There are magnificent views, especially from the viaducts of Dent Head, ten arches and 199yd long, and Arten Gill with its marginally more impressive statistics of eleven arches and a length of 220yd. Above is the summit of Great Knoutberry Hill, its name deriving from distinctive plants with strawberry-like leaves and fruits tasting of apricot wine that once grew here and are still common in Scandinavia. Knoutberry is Dales dialect for cloudberry (they were often worth 'nowt'), although few finding jam of this name on sale in Ikea will make the connection with a railway in the Dales!

Ornamental station sign at Horton-in-Ribblesdale. It was the creation of stationmaster Jim Taylor, who for 17 successive years won the 'Best Kept Garden' competition until he was transferred to Settle in 1959. Author's collection

Remnants of snow fences herald the approach to Dent station, the highest on an English main line at 1,145ft. The stationmaster's house was a pioneer in the use of double-glazing and three of its outside walls are covered by slates to provide additional insulation. Other buildings were once used as a shelter and canteen for snow-clearing crews. Dent village is a full four miles away and road access involves a corkscrew climb of 450ft from the valley bottom in little more than half a mile on a gradient of 1 in 5. The road was still rough and unmetalled in the 1950s and villagers must have found it as easy to go to Sedbergh on the Ingleton to Low Gill line, only a little further and involving far less exertion. It says much that in the 45 years from opening until the 1923 grouping, Dent station apparently issued only one season ticket.

The second of two major tunnels on the line is 1,213yd Rise Hill, taking it onto another shelf above the straight and not-so-green Garsdale. This brief level stretch, rarely photographed owing to its inaccessibility, permitted the installation in 1907 of the world's highest water troughs. They were fed by a 43,000-gallon storage tank that collected the abundant rainwater falling on the surrounding fells and for many years was steam-heated by a coal-fired boiler in the winter months. Harassed firemen nevertheless claimed that the troughs were frozen in winter, dry in summer, blocked by leaves in autumn and thus only of use in spring.

Railway cottages cluster close to what is now Garsdale station (originally named Hawes Junction). It was rather more than the divergence point of the Hawes branch, closed in 1959, as it was also the point where pilot engines that had been detached after assisting trains up the banks from either Hellifield or Carlisle were turned before working back to their respective depots. They used what arguably became Britain's most famous turntable, surrounded by a stockade of sleepers after an incident in December 1900 when an engine caught by a freak wind was sent whirling round like a spinning top.

Special features of the railway community included a social centre under an 80,000 gallon water tank. Complete with piano and stage, it was used prior to the coming of TV for concerts, dances, potato pie suppers and domino and whist drives. In one of the waiting rooms there was a solemn ceremony on Sundays when a portable organ was wheeled into place for divine service. A register recorded items lost and found, which ranged widely and embraced a retriever dog left without its owner, a basket of rhubarb, a parcel of clogs, two butcher's knives and three ploughshares!

Beyond Garsdale station is the twelve-arch Dandry Mire viaduct, only built after a quarter of a million tons of earth had been tipped in an unsuccessful attempt to form an embankment. Up to this point the Settle–Carlisle has been running on relatively gentle undulating gradients all the way from Blea Moor, but it now begins its final climb through the short Moorcock and Shotlock Hill tunnels to Ais Gill, at 1,169ft the highest summit on an English main line. Here England's most spectacular railway leaves the Dales and passes 2,324ft Wild Boar Fell to begin its long descent down the Eden Valley.

Men at work

THE Settle–Carlisle has become famous as the last of the great trunk routes to be almost wholly dependent on the railway navvy for its creation. At the peak of construction in the summer of 1871 the workforce on the whole line numbered almost 7,000 men. Mechanical aids included tramways with attendant locomotives, tip wagons, fixed steam engines at the head of tunnel shafts and mobile cranes for erecting the viaducts. Dynamite, then a novelty, was brought in by road as an alternative to the traditional but more dangerous use of gunpowder. Over 500 horses were also employed by the various contractors, but there was none of the wholesale dependence on the steam excavator that was to characterise construction of the Great Central Railway two decades later.

On the windswept and treeless upper section of the route, which had hitherto remained almost immune from human settlement, a major problem was provision of accommodation for the navvies. Shanty towns appeared at

Ribblehead station is 1,025ft above sea level and prone to weather extremes.
It appropriately became an official meteorological reporting point in 1938 and
Stationmaster Clark is seen releasing a hydrogen balloon to determine cloud cover.
Geoffrey N.Wright

many places and had colourful names such as Jericho, Inkerman, Sebastopol,
Salt Lake City and Belgravia. The largest and most famous was Batty Green at
Ribblehead. Its often overcrowded and rat-infested wooden huts housed some
2,000 men, women and children, and a vast assortment of domestic animals.
Reminiscent of something out of the American Mid-West, this was a complete
community with shops, an abundance of ale houses, a hospital, post office,
bakery, slaughter house, library, mission house and day and Sunday schools.
There were also stables, stores, workshops, a brickworks and a sawmill.

Contractors offered high wages and piece-rate working but navvies would
often stop working in the afternoon when they felt they had earned enough

and would constantly drift away in search of an easier livelihood. In a two-pronged approach to maintaining harmony, both scripture readers and policemen were appointed to watch over the workforce. The men were a potentially explosive mixture of English, Irish and Scots resulting in many deaths from inebriation and wild living. There were also fatal outbreaks of smallpox and the tiny graveyards at Chapel-le-Dale church, west of Batty Green, and at Cowgill in Dentdale had to be extended.

In autumn 1871 the contractor responsible for the first 17 miles of line northwards from Settle got into financial difficulties. The Midland took over the work itself, and now became directly aware of the almost superhuman problems involved in building a railway through such challenging countryside. The weather was unusually bad, even by the standards of the high Dales, with 92 inches of rain being recorded at Dent Head in 1872 compared with an average of 68 inches. Boulder clay turned to slurry and it was necessary to use bog carts with their frame resting on a huge barrel instead of conventional wheels. The inhospitable climate with its howling gales, near-horizontal blizzards and persistent low cloud proved too much on top of delays already caused by a fickle labour force. When construction began in 1869 there was every confidence that the line would be open four years later, but the date was constantly pushed back until the first passenger services finally ran in 1876.

Wild weather

THE conditions during the building of the line were a steep learning curve. It would be hard to find a better example of prosaic railway phraseology than in the LMS General Appendix: 'Stationmasters and signalmen between Hellifield and Carlisle must carefully watch the weather during the winter months'. It conjures up a half-humorous picture of men perpetually staring at scudding clouds, but in fact the warning was written in the light of continuing bitter experience. In the days of 'proper' winters, snowploughs were stationed in readiness and snow fences constructed on the most exposed parts of the line. An additional problem was dangerous icicles of monstrous size forming inside the tunnels.

An engraving in F.S. Williams' classic history of the Midland Railway depicts an engine snowed up near Dent with only the top of its chimney protruding through the drift. It might be thought an exaggeration, but just such an incident occurred during a 1933 blizzard that closed the line for almost a week. A locomotive disappeared beneath the snow and was only located by digging down until a spade made a metallic clang.

In the winter of 1947 it snowed for two months and the wind blew day and

Garsdale water troughs on one of the few level stretches on the Settle–Carlisle.
Keeping them free of ice in a harsh winter could be nigh impossible, although the tank
that fed them had a coal-fired boiler. Geoffrey G. Hoare

night. The line was blocked for no less than eight weeks in February and
March when the buildings on the up platform at Dent ceased to be visible.
A task force of 500 men included soldiers of the East Lancashire Regiment
and Italian prisoners of war, but a combined assault with snowploughs and
even a jet engine had little effect on drifts up to twelve feet deep and half a mile
long that had turned to ice. Locomotives frozen onto Garsdale water troughs
were eventually removed, and when one track was reopened the railway
became a lifeline for remote farms in upper Ribblesdale and Dentdale by
transporting foodstuffs and hay. It was early April before normal services were
fully restored.

The line was again blocked for almost a week in January 1963 when the
Edinburgh to London sleeper became stranded in a drift south of Rise Hill
tunnel. It proved possible to transfer passengers to the last three carriages and
a heroic crew worked these back to Carlisle with an engine running tender-first
into the teeth of a blizzard.

In both 1947 and 1963 through trains were diverted via Ingleton and
the West Coast main line, an option that ceased to be available with closure
of the link between Clapham and Low Gill in 1966. On today's railway the
preferred course is bus substitution or outright cancellation. There is a certain

irony that by far the longest cessation of through services has been caused not by snow but by rain and consequent flooding, and moreover has occurred on the more sylvan reaches of the line in the Eden Valley outside the Dales. The horrendous Storm Desmond of December 2015 caused subsidence that two months later resulted in closure of the railway north of Armathwaite throughout 2016.

Life at Blea Moor

LIFE for railwaymen and their families living on the upper reaches of the line could be harsh. One of those who has recorded vivid memories is Nancy Edmondson, whose father accepted the sub-ganger's post at Blea Moor in 1939. It involved moving into a cottage supplied with water from the same tank used to replenish locomotives. Coal for the kitchen-cum-living room came courtesy of firemen's shovels and lighting was by paraffin lamps and candles. Nancy and her two elder sisters became known as the Blea Moor railway children.

They would often keep an eye on things in the signal-box while the signalman went for a swim in the water tank. School involved a walk of over a mile to Ribblehead and they would sometimes have to load the hems of their coats with small stones in an effort to avoid becoming airborne. On occasions it was necessary to take shelter behind one of the viaduct piers and then make a dash for it during a lull in the gale.

On Tuesdays, Nancy's mother would catch a train at Ribblehead to shop in Settle and, providing the crew knew her, the return service would make an unofficial stop at Blea Moor so that she could jump down to the trackside. This kind of travel moved up a notch when elder sister Edith got married and left home with bridal dress over her arm, riding on the footplate of a goods engine brought to an unscheduled halt at the signals. She was deposited at Ribblehead station to change into her finery prior to the wedding at Chapel-le-Dale church. Nancy's other sister went one better, married to a signalman and living in a house at Blea Moor. She went into labour unexpectedly early with the result that an express was stopped so she could be heaved on board to get to the maternity hospital in Skipton.

The most memorable of all days at Blea Moor occurred on an April afternoon in 1952. Nancy was sunbathing on top of the pigsty when suddenly there was a tremendous crash. The up Thames–Clyde Express derailed with one of its two locomotives toppling on its side and three carriages rearing up before crashing back sideways over the running lines.

Apart from the signalman, who immediately summoned help, she and her mum were the only people on the scene and their home became a casualty clearing station. When rescuers eventually arrived, they were appalled to find bodies littering the embankment but they turned out to be passengers who had given all possible help and were recovering in the sun.

Changing times

NANCY Edmondson was living in what now seems a totally different world. Going back further, hill farmers used to just bleating sheep and horse-drawn carts must have rubbed their eyes in disbelief when Midland expresses began to pound their way over the desolate heights of the Settle–Carlisle. It would be akin to the first aeroplane landing on the foothills of the Himalayas. Determined to offer superior standards of comfort, the company had imported both parlour and sleeping Pullman cars from the USA. With their all-American outline, nothing quite like them had previously been seen in Britain. They headed their exotic way from London to such destinations as Glasgow, Edinburgh, Inverness and Stranraer for the Larne boat but were often running non-stop between Leeds and Carlisle and stations in the Dales were simply beneath their dignity.

Local traffic was never more than minimal and even in a peak year such as 1910 there were only four stopping services each way. The gradual decline that began on formation of the LMS in 1923 and continued into BR days saw one small improvement with the end of steam haulage. Drivers had never been keen to stop on the gradient at Settle, but this was not a problem with diesel power and the town at last enjoyed fast services to both Leeds and Carlisle.

By this time a question mark was starting to hang over the future of the line, and to realists there was some surprise that it had not been abandoned in favour of the shorter Ingleton route with its lower maintenance costs. Policy statements of the 1960s proposed closure for passengers with just 'sidings' left at either end for mineral traffic. An application to withdraw local services and close all stations in the Dales apart from Settle was refused by the Minister of Transport in 1964. Matters then seemed to be taking a turn for the better when 'paytrains' operated by diesel multiple units were introduced in April 1966, but it proved a short-lived reprieve with the station closures finally taking effect in May 1970. Where there was little habitation in sight it was difficult to argue with the conclusion that 'very severe hardship would be caused to very few people'.

The wheel of fortune that was to create uncertainty for the next two decades then had an upswing. Electrification of the West Coast main line in the early 1970s highlighted the difficulty of interlacing slow freight trains with high-speed expresses. It was decided that retention of the Settle–Carlisle was

Photographers were favoured by rare fortune when a patch of sunlight followed A4 No.4498 *Sir Nigel Gresley* as it crossed Ribblehead viaduct on 28 November 1981. It was the year when it was announced that the structure would either have to be replaced or the line closed, although neither were destined to happen. Gavin Morrison

Ribblehead viaduct under construction. This painting by Alan Fearnley depicts the difficult working conditions with pick and shovel the only means of battling against boulder clay. A contractor's locomotive is conveying timber for use in supporting the arches. Author's collection

The lonely railway settlement at Blea Moor (an appropriate dialect corruption of 'bleak').
It is remote from road access and life could be challenging for its inhabitants.
The signal-box on the left is now widely seen as the most remote in England. W.R. Mitchell

essential for freight and diversionary purposes, and many improvements including extensive track relaying now took place. Symptomatic of the new era was the success of Dales Rail, the collaboration between British Rail and the Yorkshire Dales National Park which in the summer of 1975 saw the reopening of intermediate stations for weekend charter trains from Leeds. They brought walkers into the Dales and return workings enabled local residents to have a day out in the big city.

The fare structure was designed to encourage visitors to travel into the National Park by rail instead of road and, as additional attractions, guided walks were provided from several of the stations with connecting bus services also being arranged from Garsdale to Sedbergh and Hawes. A total of 10,000 passenger journeys were made during the twelve days of the service which had an operating surplus. During 1976, Dales Rail trains were also introduced from Manchester, Preston and Clitheroe.

Contrary to gloomy predictions of only a few years earlier, England's highest and most spectacular main line had survived to celebrate its centenary. The mood of optimism was heightened in 1978 when BR agreed to a limited return of steam specials to the line, culminating in the Cumbrian Mountain Express and invasions of photographers by the hundred. The euphoria was perhaps too good to last and in 1981 came a bombshell that was to create intense media scrutiny and excitement for the next nine years.

Closure by stealth?

THE events of the 1980s represent successful opposition to closure proposals on a scale that has never been equalled and hopefully will not be required again. The 'cat-and-mouse' game is now tending to fade into the past but should not be forgotten.

Early in 1981 it was announced that Ribblehead viaduct was deteriorating to such an extent that it would either have to be replaced within five years or the line closed. The following year most express services were diverted away from the Settle–Carlisle in a move that brought widespread allegations of 'dirty tricks'. Leaked documents showed that traffic was being removed in order to claim the line was not needed. All that was left were just two trains each way between Leeds and Carlisle which continued to call at Settle. Fears that this was the beginning of the end were heightened in August 1983 with official publication of closure plans.

The Settle–Carlisle had still to achieve cult status but there was suddenly truth in the old adage that an Englishman never fully appreciates anything until he is about to lose sight of it. Nothing quite like the resulting outcry had ever been seen. Had the approach taken by British Rail smacked less of what was described as 'closure by stealth', the opposition might not have been quite so determined. As it was, events led to the formation of the successful Friends of the Settle–Carlisle Line. It joined forces with other groups as part of the highly professional Settle–Carlisle Joint Action Committee, which broke new ground by becoming a limited company with full-time staff. By the end of the statutory period the number of objectors to closure totalled an unprecedented 22,150 – with the addition of one dog signing the petition to save the line with his paw print.

A curious twist in the saga was the October 1983 appointment by BR of Ron Cotton as the line's project manager. His brief was to see through closure but he proved to be a flawed choice. Primarily an innovative marketing man, he brought such an upsurge in passengers that the two regular trains soon extended from four to as many as eleven carriages. By the spring of 1985 there were three services each way with the morning train from Leeds to Carlisle sometimes running in triplicate. His next move the following year was to support local authorities in the reopening on a daily basis of inter-mediate stations previously used only at weekends by Dales Rail. The supreme paradox was that they now had the best service they had ever enjoyed. This paved the way for a further increase to five trains each way, the result being that the six years to 1989 saw passenger journeys increase from 93,000 to 450,000 per annum.

5MT No.44669 heads past deep drifts at Dent station on 26 January 1963 – the first day the line had been reopened after a blockage of almost a week. An overnight sleeper train was stranded between here and Rise Hill tunnel. Gavin Morrison

The bleak scene at Dent just a few days before the above photograph with hand-shovelling of snow in progress. Jack Sedgewick

The return of steam specials over the Settle–Carlisle from 1978 hugely increased interest in the line. Heading a long 14-carriage train, No.46229 *Duchess of Hamilton* is still dwarfed by its surroundings when crossing Dandry Mire viaduct on 29 October 1983. Gavin Morrison

While these positive developments were taking place, British Rail and its opponents remained locked in conflict with report following report and rumour being heaped upon rumour. A bleak moment finally came in May 1988 when the then Transport Minister, David Mitchell, announced to a hostile House of Commons that he was 'minded to consent' to closure, although a final decision would be delayed to allow time for a private bidder to come forward with proposals to run a preserved railway.

This attempt to use the line as a test bed for privatisation foundered, but even so objectors were taken off-guard by the sudden announcement in April 1989 that the Secretary of State for Transport was refusing closure. British Rail put on a brave face, proclaiming it welcomed the decision because it removed uncertainty, and began a major programme of repairs. These had as their first priority Ribblehead viaduct, the structure that eight years earlier had triggered this extraordinary sequence of events. Long overdue renewal of the

Sheriff Brow viaduct

bridge deck waterproofing was followed by skilful replacement of decayed stonework, with fiberglass moulds being used to make the outer facing resemble the original.

Usage now continued to increase with passenger numbers reaching 1.2 million in 2012. New facilities include a special visitor centre at Ribblehead station, where the down platform has been restored. It had been removed in 1974 to make way for a siding to handle ballast brought up by road from a quarry near Ingleton. Apart from leisure traffic, an important development in January 2016 was the reopening of rail access to Arcow and Dry Rigg quarries at Horton-in-Ribblesdale. It has enabled stone to be taken out of the Yorkshire Dales National Park in trains weighing up to 2,000 tonnes instead of by road.

More than a quarter of century has elapsed since the reprieve of the Settle–Carlisle and it is dangerously easy to take its future for granted. Graphically illustrating this position is the fact that repairing the 2015 landslip in the Eden Valley cost a frightening £23 million. Even allowing for inflation, this is significantly more than 1981 estimates ranging up to £6 million for replacing Ribblehead viaduct. Such sums were then deemed prohibitively expensive and cited both politically and economically as a prime reason for closure. It was a stance that those seeking to safeguard the line must always remember.

Chapter Four

Swaledale

THE railway age in Swaledale was a more straightforward affair than in the other major dales. A short branch line to its gateway town of Richmond opened in 1846 and grew old gradually before closing after a life of 123 years. Yet in one respect it was outstanding – its terminus was like no other. A product of the golden age of railway architecture, it was happily completed just before collapse of the Mania period forced a cutback in many grand projects.

It was also fortunate that the Richmond branch formed part of the empire of George Hudson, who despite his many malpractices never cut corners with his stations. He firmly believed in helping those who helped him, one of whom was the architect George Townsend Andrews. The two men respectively became Lord Mayor and High Sheriff of York, and it was Andrews who contrived to have Hudson's nominees returned to Parliament unopposed in the 1847 general election. Favours had already been exchanged and the 'railway king' gave Andrews a free rein in creating stations both to please and to endure. At Richmond he excelled himself.

Local sandstone was plentiful and it was used to create a terminus described as 'monastic Gothic', astonishingly medieval with its cloister-like entrance, mullioned windows and tall angled chimneys. A distinctive two-bay trainshed in glass and iron covered the platforms and its gable ends were decorated with herringbone timbering and exquisite bargeboards. Built at the same time to form a coherent whole were an engine shed, goods shed, stationmaster's house, a row of six railway cottages and a gas works of unusually elegant design for such a mundane purpose.

It was all designed to match the historic buildings in the town, which is on the opposite side of the river Swale across a substantial stone bridge built by the railway company.

Inevitably there were problems with such an ambitious concept and the station was not opened until 9 April 1847, seven months after the first trains

Early photograph of Richmond station about 1865. The locomotive is a 2-2-2.
Ken Hoole collection

arrived at a temporary wooden platform. One cause of delay may have been Nathaniel Plews, a Great North of England Railway director who was no fan of lavish stations. He later claimed that he had managed to get the original design scaled down, thereby incurring 'much ill will'.

When the station closed in March 1969 it had already become a Grade II★ listed building and its importance was recognised by the local authority. Three years later it purchased the whole site, and after a period as a garden centre it was leased to Richmondshire Building Preservation Trust which carried out major renovation work. In November 2007 it reopened as a community and business centre – named simply 'The Station' – complete with restaurant, art gallery, two cinema screens and a range of artisan food producers. The engine shed has become a gymnasium and the goods shed replaced by a sensitively designed swimming pool. The remarkable creation of G.T. Andrews has been brought back into the heart of Richmond and its people.

The style and panache of its terminus inevitably tends to overshadow the branch as a whole. Its initial passenger service between Darlington and Richmond began with three trains each way on weekdays and two on Sundays, this number gradually increasing and remaining at a respectable level right up until the 1969 closure. In the 1930s most services were worked by Sentinel steam railcars. Richmond station shared its busiest-ever day with Leyburn when on 29 June 1927 it was chosen by the LNER as the destination for

A century later in 1965 the distinctive gable ends of the terminus were unchanged, although only four years remained before closure. On the left is the matching stationmaster's house. David Sutcliffe

Opening of the Richmond branch cut the cost of transporting lead from the Swaledale mines to Stockton-on-Tees by about a third. Ingots are being weighed on primitive scales at the terminus circa 1870. Behind the men is the engine shed, now a gymnasium. Ken Hoole collection

excursions to see a total eclipse of the sun. In this case two sleeping car trains arrived overnight from King's Cross and there were also specials from Marylebone, King's Lynn and Edinburgh. Cloud cover proved just as disastrous as in Wensleydale.

On the freight side, traffic in lead ore that had been a major factor in promotion of the line tailed off once the Swaledale mines peaked in the 1860s. The railway still tried to please all comers, as instanced by providing a private siding on the approach to Richmond 'used by Mr Jaques, Gentleman, of Easby Hall, and his tenants for coal and an occasional wagon of manure'. Jaques & Co. played a leading role in lead extraction in Arkengarthdale and mining interests frequently tried to revive the industry by promoting a line west of Richmond at least as far as Reeth. The last attempt as late as 1912 collapsed when the necessary finance could not be obtained.

Two years later the country was at war and in 1915 the army established the massive Catterick Camp close to Richmond. A two-foot gauge line worked by Hudswell Clarke and Kerr Stuart locomotives was laid to carry materials from Catterick Bridge station, indicative of the urgency being that it shared the bridge carrying the Great North Road across the river Swale. Such an arrangement could only be temporary and it was superseded by the standard gauge Military Camp Railway with its five-mile single-track main line and various sidings serving stores and depots. As many as 45,000 men were stationed at the camp and had to suffer a passenger service using ancient North London Railway four-wheel carriages. A motley collection of loco-motives was acquired from such distant concerns as the Rhymney and Stratford-upon-Avon & Midland Junction companies.

The line remained busy through the Second World War, a tragic accident occurring in February 1944 when munitions were being loaded in the goods yard at Catterick Bridge. Twelve men were killed, 102 injured and the station buildings were badly damaged. In the line's final years there were weekend trains from Catterick Camp through to London and Bristol with return workings in the early hours of Monday mornings, provided to enable soldiers taking leave to reach their units in time for duty.

Chapter Five

Wensleydale

Features of the route

THE railway through Wensleydale from Northallerton to Hawes Junction (later Garsdale) was unique in the Dales in being built by as many as four different companies over a period of thirty years. This meant its stations had some striking architectural variety, indicative of the changing times and styles of respectively the Great North of England, Bedale & Leyburn, North Eastern and Midland railways.

The initial section that reached Leeming Lane (now Leeming Bar) in 1848 reflected the turbulent years when George Hudson was in command. His architect and political crony, George Townsend Andrews, was later criticised for the 'wanton extravagance' of his stations. This can be seen at Ainderby, the first intermediate station, which had little significance in operational terms but nevertheless boasted an ambitious split-level design with low-pitched roofs and Georgian-style sash windows.

Extravagance did not reign supreme and by contrast the next station at Scruton was a modest single-storey affair with an attractive glass-fronted waiting room. In its heyday it epitomised the country railway with the station-master having so much time to spare that the building virtually disappeared under potted plants and shrubs. It was clearly in a sheltered location, as after closure it vanished under a mountain of ivy until villagers spent over 300 hours stripping away the foliage.

Ostentation came to the fore at Leeming Lane, where the two-storey building is of classical proportions with a low-pitched slate roof. The real surprise is at the east end with its pillared portico, which is of little practical purpose but nevertheless provides a delightful final flourish. Similar structures by G.T. Andrews survive at Lockington and Nafferton on the Hull to Scarborough line. Today it seems inconceivable that the adjacent level crossing was until the 1950s part of the main A1 artery from London to Scotland, with long queues of frustrated motorists venting their fury as trains trundled past at their

The initial section of the Wensleydale railway has few major features as it heads west from Northallerton. Its first significant river crossing is at Morton, where its spans the Swale as it meanders into the Vale of York. Charter workings can add more than a touch of colour, as shown by an East Midlands HST on a charity special from St Pancras on 4 April 2013. Gavin Morrison

own pace. On the far side of the crossing a private siding served the Vale of Mowbray Bacon Factory, noted far and wide for its pork pies.

When the Bedale & Leyburn Railway was formed to continue the line westwards, it may well have inherited some of Andrews' original designs. Bedale station has architectural similarities with both Ainderby and Leeming Lane. It boasted a fine assortment of semaphore signals until the 1980s and still retains the only North Eastern Railway signal box on the branch.

Beyond this point the company optimistically decided to cram five intermediate stations into the next ten miles. Progress was woefully slow and passengers must have had to endure temporary facilities long after the 1856 opening, as it was another six years before all five were under construction. Although often remote from civilisation, this did not stop such luxuries as decorative chimneys and French-style shutters. They were made doubly incongruous by the use of stepped gables in brick rather than cheaper local stone.

Ironically, the plainest station was Leyburn itself, completed before the Bedale & Leyburn was taken over by the North Eastern in 1859. The most important settlement on the whole line had to make do with barrack-like grey

Bedale still retains the only North Eastern Railway signal box on the branch.
Passing with a special on 20 September 1992 were class 20s Nos 20169 and 20092.
Gavin Morrison

stone structures simple to the point of austerity, with the main station building resembling a farmhouse and the adjoining goods shed a barn. Only a sloping canopy originally relieved the slab-like façade. At least there was a first-floor boardroom for the company's directors, while also enhancing the station in its heyday were separate first-class waiting rooms for gentlemen and ladies, a footbridge, two signal boxes, a single-road engine shed and a 42ft turntable capable of turning most of the engines used on the branch.

By the time the Wensleydale line reached Leyburn it had climbed steadily from the low-lying Vale of York to breast the 500ft contour. Its North Eastern stations to the west reflected the more robust surroundings and also the fact that they were a later product of the 1870s. They still managed to verge on the extravagant and again were utterly at odds with the local vernacular architecture. Built in 'country cottage' style to the designs of the North Eastern's architect Thomas Prosser, an oddity was that the company imported the stone by rail rather than using local quarries.

Redmire, Aysgarth and Askrigg were virtually identical, but Wensley differed slightly in that the landowner Lord Bolton was able to insist on a private waiting room, toilet and separate entrance onto the platform for the exclusive use of his family. Trains were instructed to await the arrival of the Bolton entourage whenever they wished to travel, an arrangement that caused no end

Finghall Lane, serving a small village, reflected the optimism of the Bedale & Leyburn Railway in providing five intermediate stations on a ten-mile stretch of railway. There was also sheer extravagance with the inclusion of stepped gable ends and five chimney stacks on the main building. The staff of three clearly had ample time to tend the station gardens. Author's collection

of trouble. Aristocratic timekeeping was such that scholarship children on their way to Northallerton were often late for school, although what were classed as 'extenuating circumstances' meant they were never punished! The separate entrance onto the platform with its sign 'Lord Bolton's Waiting Room' was characteristic of a more feudal age.

Although the line has been lifted beyond Redmire, the station at Aysgarth has been purchased by the Wensleydale Railway and largely restored to pre-closure condition. It only needs tracks and trains to bring it fully back to life. Former times are also clearly evident at Hawes, where much of the station has found a new lease of life as the Dales Countryside Museum. Reflecting its origins, it provided the final touch of architectural variety and was pure Midland with its station buildings, goods shed and signal box identical to those on the Settle–Carlisle line.

At around 800ft above sea level, Hawes has long vied with Alston and Princetown on Dartmoor as the highest market town in England. The surroundings of the Wensleydale railway became more austere as it embarked on its final six miles and in quick succession encountered the three main engineering features on the entire line. These were Appersett viaduct, 125yd long with five spans, the shorter four-arch Mossdale viaduct and then the 245yd Mossdale Head Tunnel, which encountered unexpectedly hard rock during construction and delayed completion of the line.

Although the end of the Wensleydale line at Hawes Junction (now Garsdale) was very much Midland territory, there was one structure here of key importance to the North Eastern. This was a small engine shed, which the company rented at a cost of £2 per month so that it was in a position to work the first morning through train to Northallerton. It also paid an additional 9s a week for the use of three railway cottages to house enginemen and a cleaner, whose duties included 'night firing' so that the engine was always ready for its first turn of duty at around 6.30am. The shed was closed in 1939.

There were never many passengers using this upper section of line, but those few often had to brave the elements when they reached Hawes Junction, well above the 1,000ft contour. Other cross-country railways have begun and ended in radically different surroundings, but few have terminated in a location that could be grim beyond belief when the weather was at its worst. Rather than watching an engine struggling to turn on the unique stockaded turntable, passengers probably took immediate refuge in the waiting room. Here at least there was a small library thoughtfully established by two travellers who had been becalmed in this loneliest of railway outposts.

Handling the traffic

THE Wensleydale line was favoured with more than its fair share of scenic attractions. A local guide published just before its final completion forecast:

> The district is rich in natural advantages – in beautiful scenery, in many magnificent views and in romantic historical associations. It is probable that one of the chief sources of traffic will be that drawn to it by the desire to see its natural beauties.

The prediction soon proved correct, the basic service of four or five trains each way carrying not just local people but also tourists who for the first time came to the upper dale in substantial numbers. Apart from Aysgarth Falls, they also enthused over Bolton Castle and Hardraw Force, near Hawes, the setting for a famous annual Brass Band Contest. This came to attract thousands of spectators from far afield, a typical year being 1903 when excursion trains headed into the dale from Manchester, Leeds, York, Saltburn, Hartlepool and Newcastle.

Edwardian travellers were nothing if not stoical. In September of the same year an excursion offering a very full day at the seaside left Northallerton at the

Above: Never specially attractive, Leyburn station was unusual in that the main building on the right is on the goods platform and the more distant goods shed is alongside the main passenger platform. In its heyday the austere station façade was relieved by a glass canopy running almost its full length. J.W. Armstrong Trust

Opposite, top: The canopy was dismantled following closure to passengers in 1954 but the peculiar kink in the platform is still clearly visible. Class 60 no.60030 is passing on 16 December 1992 with a train of empties for Redmire during the last week of stone traffic. Gavin Morrison

Lower: Reopening by the Wensleydale Railway Company in 2003 has brought a considerable improvement in appearance. A class 110 diesel unit is alongside the now straight platform on 17 October 2009. Gavin Morrison

unearthly hour of 4.50am and, after calling at various stations in the dale, finally reached Morecambe just after 9am. The return journey did not commence until 7.45pm and there must surely have been many a sleepy head on a train that finally dragged itself back into Northallerton after midnight.

Scenic excursions by rail were very much a feature between the wars, with Wensleydale an obvious choice of route. Trains would head north from York before going up the dale through Leyburn and Hawes and then down the Settle–Carlisle line to Appleby. Return was over the dramatic Stainmore route through Barnard Castle to Darlington, from whence York was regained via the East Coast main line.

The largest ever influx of passengers onto the branch occurred on 29 June 1927, when it was thought that Leyburn would be one of the best centres in England to view a total eclipse of the sun. No fewer than eight special trains

Changing trains at windswept Hawes
Junction could often be a bleak experience
for Wensleydale line passengers. Renamed
Garsdale in 1932, the station did at least have
a small library in its waiting room.
The stationmaster is seen selecting
a book in 1945. Author's collection

arrived from points as distant as London and Norwich, the sheer numbers proving a major operating headache for local railway staff. Sadly it all ended in anti-climax, with cloud cover being such that participants saw nothing other than a brief darkening of the sky.

The Wensleydale line was unusual in that milk traffic vied with handling passengers in its importance. The rich pastures of the dale had been a fertile home for dairy cattle since monastic times, although until the coming of the railway the milk was largely turned into butter and cheese for local consumption. It could now instead be sent to distant towns and cities, and by the early 1900s over 10,000 gallons a week was leaving the line in large churns conveyed in special vans. Other dairy products continued to be important, with the afternoon Midland goods being instructed to 'wait at Hawes till the butter is ready on Tuesdays'!

The North Eastern and later the LNER did everything possible to encourage milk traffic, aiding the establishment of dairies close to Redmire and Northallerton stations. The heyday came in the 1920s and early '30s, when seven days a week a D17 4-4-0 would outshine normal motive power on the branch and head out light engine all the way from Northallerton to Hawes to work a 'fast' milk train. This left Hawes at 7pm and called at Askrigg and Leyburn, the milk reaching Finsbury Park at 2.55am in time for bottling to form the morning 'pinta' for London's inhabitants. The LMS in turn kept the west end of the line open on Sundays by daily operating two milk trains out of

Right: Hawes was a joint North Eastern and Midland station. Architecturally it was pure Midland with all its buildings identical to those on the Settle–Carlisle line. One of the last through passenger trains along the Wensleydale railway was this Leeds Publicity Club special on 6 September 1958, six months before complete closure of the line to Garsdale. Much of the station now forms part of the Dales Countryside Museum. Author's collection

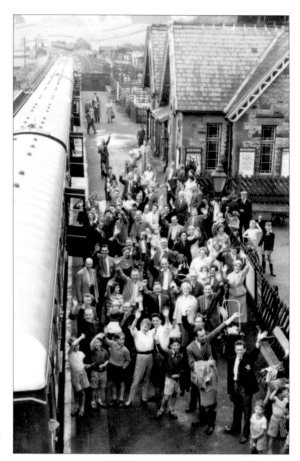

Below: Entrance to the 245yd Mossdale Head Tunnel, one of the few major engineering works on the line. J.W. Armstrong Trust

Hawes. Traffic over the Wensleydale railway continued to increase following the opening in 1937 of a rail-connected Express Dairy at Leyburn, which two years later achieved an all-time annual peak in dispatching 3,200,000 gallons, mainly to a depot in Cricklewood.

Leyburn was also especially noted as a centre of horse-breeding and training. The station handled some 2,000 horses per annum in the early years of the twentieth century, with complete horsebox specials to the various race meetings being a regular occurrence. All stations had considerable livestock traffic, sometimes not without incident as happened at Askrigg when a bullock broke loose and promptly headed through the front door of a nearby cottage before scrambling upstairs to the bedroom. History does not relate what happened next!

The outward traffic over the line that ultimately became the most significant started in the early days, as shown in 1889 when the Midland conveyed over 13,000 tons of locally quarried building stone from Hawes. Much of it was of high quality, but little was wasted and inferior material was reputedly used as casings for manhole covers on London's expanding sewerage system. Output was soon eclipsed by stone of a different kind and in 1908 a siding was installed to serve a limestone quarry at Harmby, east of Leyburn. Further sidings were provided for quarries west of Leyburn as well as at Wensley and Redmire, this traffic developing over the years to the extent that it was ultimately to prove the saviour of the branch.

Traffic variety at Leyburn

Left: In days long before yellow lines on platform edges, crowds throng the station on 29 June 1927 waiting to return home on eight special trains. They had anticipated a spectacular total eclipse of the sun but Dales weather denied them the experience. On the right are catering vehicles and gas tanks for replenishing restaurant car kitchens. H.C. Casserley

Above: Milk traffic was always important on the Wensleydale line – and intensified following the opening of an Express Dairy at Leyburn in 1937. Class Y3 Sentinel no.68182 is shunting milk tankers on 27 February 1954. J.W. Armstrong Trust

Below: Horses were handled in large numbers, one memorable occasion occurring on 19 March 1946 when Armstrong's stable was removed from Middleham to Newmarket. The LNER provided both road and rail horseboxes. Pendragon Collection

The last day of through passenger services on 26 April 1954. Class J21 No.65038 –
complete with floral wreath – is preparing to leave Garsdale. J.W. Armstrong Trust

Downward spiral

By the late 1930s there were already signs that the best years were over with
sales of passenger tickets greatly reduced compared with the position only
twenty years earlier. There was a fillip during the Second World War when
heavily laden trains brought troops, equipment and stores to military camps
concentrated in the Leeming area. Thereafter it was a story of gradual decline,
many of the intermediate stations sealing their own demise by being remote
from the villages they were supposed to serve. These communities often had as
few as two hundred inhabitants and the Wensleydale line shared the fate of
other branches in the Yorkshire Dales with closure proposals being put forward
well before the Beeching era.

British Railways announced in 1953 that it proposed to withdraw passenger
services, thus saving £14,500 per annum. It maintained that trains were used
by only 2.5% of the local community and then only once or twice a year.
Wensleydale inhabitants put up a strenuous fight but stood little chance of
success in the face of such a damning statistic. It was nevertheless a black
day in April 1954 when the full passenger service ended. The last train was
hauled by a J21 0-6-0, representing a class that along with D20 4-4-0s and
G5 0-4-4Ts had for many years provided the staple motive power. Special
trains for Aysgarth School at Newton-le-Willows continued to head up the
branch as far as Jervaulx station and there were also occasional steam-hauled
rail tours working through to Garsdale until complete closure of the western
extremity of the line beyond Hawes in March 1959.

Continuing retrenchment brought the decision to retain the eastern portion of the Wensleydale railway for the profitable limestone traffic from the largest surviving quarry at Redmire but eliminate the smaller goods yards that produced little revenue. Aysgarth, Askrigg and Hawes fell into this category and so the line was closed completely beyond Redmire in April 1964. Goods facilities at Ainderby and Leeming Bar were withdrawn in November 1965 and at Wensley in July 1967, leaving Bedale, Leyburn and Redmire as the only freight depots.

Against all odds the line then managed to continue as a half-forgotten country branch complete with manual signals and fully-staffed level crossings. A pick-up goods made its way up to Redmire and there were even some passenger trains. In the late 1970s the Yorkshire Dales National Park organised weekend 'Dalesrail' excursions that served a dual purpose in a similar way to those introduced on the Settle–Carlisle line. A DMU first took Wensleydale residents from Redmire to York for a day's sightseeing and shopping. It then returned later in the morning, bringing visitors from the city for a day out in the countryside. In the late afternoon a second return trip took the visitors back to York and finally brought the local folk home.

Rationalisation did not rear its ugly head until the early 1980s. Freight facilities at Bedale and Leyburn were closed in May 1982, finally bringing an end to the 'pick-up' goods. Signalling was removed and all signal boxes closed other than Bedale, which remained in use solely to control the crossing gates. The branch was now just a long siding, existing solely to serve the quarry at Redmire.

In this new guise the future at first seemed secure with demand for limestone remaining buoyant. By the end of the 1980s a daily 2,000-tonne train was taking 33 hopper wagons through to British Steel at Redcar. Newly built Class 60 locomotives took over the service at the end of 1990, completing what appeared to be transformation of the line. This rosy era was destined not to last. The handling facilities at Redmire were outmoded, wagons having to be loaded in three short sidings and relying on gravity shunting.

Early in 1992 British Steel revealed that it intended to cease using the Wensleydale branch and instead obtain its supplies of limestone from other sources. Events now moved ahead remorselessly with the last stone train, complete with a 'Redmire Requiem' headboard, running on 18 December 1992. Three charter passenger trains followed in the nature of a commemorative wake, as it seemed that the branch had finally breathed its last and was about to be consigned to history. Eleven years were to elapse before the preserved Wensleydale Railway was to launch a new era by carrying passengers between Leeming Bar and Leyburn.

Chapter Six

Masham and Colsterdale

MASHAM has the same river Ure as upper Wensleydale but in many ways is quite separate from the higher reaches of the valley. With the failure in the late 1860s of a proposed line linking Ripon with Leyburn via Masham, it seemed that the town was going to be one of the last remaining centres on the edge of the Dales to be denied rail access. Apart from Leyburn, such facilities were already enjoyed by Richmond, Pateley Bridge, Ilkley and Skipton. There must have been relief when in 1870 the North Eastern Railway finally agreed to build a branch from the Leeds to Thirsk and Northallerton line at Melmerby. Single track with optimistic provision for a second line of rails, it was completed five years later at a cost of a little under £37,000 [2016 = £3,140,000]. Its passenger services settled down to four each way per day normally working between Masham and Ripon with the first morning train running through to Harrogate. Bradshaw soon noted in its timetables that the branch terminus served the stately home of Swinton Park and the scenic splendours of Hack Fall, although how much extra traffic this generated is questionable.

The line might in fact have remained bereft of special interest had the town of Masham not stood at the foot of Colsterdale. Through this lesser-known dale flowed the river Burn, a tributary of the Ure, with its gathering ground on the watershed with upper Nidderdale. Just as thirsty Bradford seized on the headwaters of the Nidd for reservoir construction, so did Harrogate and Leeds obtain powers in 1901 for similar extraction from the Burn and its tributary becks.

First in the field was Harrogate with Roundhill Reservoir, six miles south-west of Masham. It was quickly evident that traction engines hauling construction materials were playing havoc with local roads and a two-foot gauge railway

Masham station about 1880 with North Eastern Railway 2-4-0ST No.84 heading the branch train. There appears to be no shortage of railway staff! NRM 6/01

The neat-looking *Leeds No. 1* supplied by Hunslet in 1905 for the two-foot gauge line from Masham station to Leighton Reservoir. It is here hauling timbers for use on site. T.E. Rounthwaite collection

was accordingly opened in 1903 from an exchange siding at Masham station. It featured some spectacular timber-trestle viaducts and was initially worked by three saddle tanks built by the Leeds firm of T. Green & Son.

Work at Roundhill was essentially complete by 1911, but siting problems delayed Leeds from making significant progress with the adjacent Leighton Reservoir until 1908. The same narrow gauge railway was used to bring men and materials up from Masham and three years earlier a powerful Hunslet 0-6-2T named *Leeds No. 1* had been purchased in readiness at a cost of £1,175 [2016 = £114,000]. Workers were housed in a timber-built village with accommodation for 400, complete with its own hospital, chapel, mission room, recreation hall and school. A 'Shoppers' Mail' ran down to Masham on Saturdays using two knifeboard carriages.

There was a radical change on the outbreak of World War I when the entire village was commandeered by the military for use first as an army camp and then for housing German officer prisoners of war. The railway continued in operation, but it was the early 1920s before reservoir construction fully resumed with Leighton finally being completed in December 1929. A delightful narrow gauge railway then fell into disuse and was lifted between April 1932 and March 1933. It was the end of an era at Masham, emphasised by the loss of its passenger services in 1931.

Military involvement was to have a second coming, as in 1941 the sole intermediate station of West Tanfield found itself serving a massive store for ammunition and other wartime 'nasties'. Traffic at the station peaked at 76,000 tons in 1944 and 42 special trains were run in the six weeks preceding D-Day. After the war, more specials were dispatched to Stranraer carrying mustard gas canisters and shells for dumping in the sea.

Thereafter the branch settled into quiet decline handling a variety of local goods and produce including malt for the town's famous breweries. It only hit the headlines in November 1962 when the MP for Darlington complained in the House of Commons that the line was being kept open solely to supply freshwater to crossing gatehouses and coal to be sold by the Masham stationmaster. Freight services, often consisting of just a couple of wagons and a brake van, lasted for only another year.

Chapter Seven

Nidderdale

Branch line to Pateley Bridge

NIDDERDALE featured in a scheme from the dawn of the railway age. Like many such ventures it had it roots in a canal proposal, when the noted engineer Thomas Telford was commissioned in 1818 to survey a route from the river Ouse to the then flax-spinning centre of Knaresborough. It proved too expensive, and so Telford was asked to look at an alternative double-track railway to the town from the river Wharfe at Bolton Percy, which would then continue as a single line to Pateley Bridge. It too failed to find sufficient support and was taken no further. With an overall length of some 28 miles, what could have claimed to be the first public railway in England was just too ambitious and ahead of its time.

There were no further proposals until the Railway Mania, when the embryo Leeds & Thirsk Railway obtained powers in 1848 to construct a branch from a junction north of Harrogate to Pateley Bridge. Straitened times meant it was never built and the railhead for the next fourteen years was Nidd Bridge station, near Ripley and alongside the turnpike road from Knaresborough. At least it meant coal could now be bought for about 10s a ton, half the price quoted in 1820. Following opening of the Leeds & Thirsk throughout in July 1849, the 'Nidderdale Omnibus' operated twice daily in connection with the trains and completed the journey to Pateley Bridge in about two hours. The single fare was 2s 0d inside and 1s 6d outside – a princely sum for a working population on average wages of little more than six shillings a week.

Continuing pressure for a branch line up the dale was led by 'industrial squire' George Metcalfe, owner of Glasshouses Mill. It was only after the 1854 formation of the North Eastern Railway that he was successful and local interests still had to raise capital amounting to £40,000. Once construction was finally started by Messrs Cail & Towns of Newcastle in September 1860, the line was soon completed in readiness for opening in May 1862. It had no special engineering features apart from two crossings of the river Nidd and

Dacre, about 1908, looking towards Pateley Bridge. It was the busiest intermediate station on the branch and handled timber, agricultural produce and high-grade sand as well as serving a sizeable village. T.J. Edgington collection

no gradients steeper than 1 in 110. Designed by the North Eastern Railway architect Thomas Prosser, all the initial stations were of the style still to be seen at Goathland on the North Yorkshire Moors Railway. It is noted for its chunky stepped gables and prominent bay window, although a drawback was the lack of any covered platform area. At Pateley Bridge this was overcome by the provision of an unusual glazed conservatory,

Four passenger trains ran daily to and from Harrogate and on Wednesdays there were two market-day services each way to Knaresborough. The Metcalfe family were devout Methodists and it no doubt delighted them that there were no trains on Sundays. Some of the Pateley Bridge inhabitants would certainly need a day of rest, for as famously related by the author E.L. Ahrons they would on a Saturday night quench their thirst in Harrogate to such an extent that the last train home would be missed. Happily the line was then worked by two ancient 2-4-0s, memorable for 'the possession of the most ear-piercing and blood-curdling whistles that probably ever adorned a British locomotive'. It appears that an arrangement was made for the crew to sound the well-known shriek in time for revellers to pour out of the pubs and thus avoid a long walk up Nidderdale in the night hours.

An immediate benefit of the railway was that freight charges for coal fell to around 5*s* per ton and made steam power in the local mills an economic proposition. It also lowered the transport costs of yarn and raw materials. There were similar benefits to the dale's agriculture with a siding being provided at Pateley Bridge to serve the corn mill. Greater emphasis on dairy farming became evident, as there was a ready market for liquid milk in the growing industrial towns of the West Riding.

The once rich veins of lead around Greenhow Hill above Nidderdale had largely been exhausted by the mid-nineteenth century, but the railway enabled this source of traffic to be superseded by high-quality stone from local quarries. This was already being taken down dale to Nidd Bridge as soon as the Leeds & Thirsk opened, although its sheer weight made transport an arduous task. Rail access to Pateley Bridge immediately overcame the problem with local historian William Grainge noting in 1861 that the stone flags were now being 'extensively used for landings and for the platforms of railway stations, where great extent of surface and durability are required'.

It was again George Metcalfe who spearheaded the development of stone quarrying. At Pateley Bridge the branch continued from the passenger terminus across the main road to sidings, from where a 1,000yd-long self-acting incline was built in 1871–73 to Scot Gate Ash Quarry above the east side of the valley. Its gradient varied from 1 in 3 to 1 in 11. By September 1873, Metcalfe was employing more than 150 workers at the quarry and had installed steam cranes running on 10ft gauge rails. Apart from station platforms all over the country, the output was also used for such noteworthy buildings as Victoria station and the National Gallery in London. Also active at this time were marble quarries higher up the dale near Lofthouse, with an abortive proposal being made to build a connecting railway to Pateley Bridge.

Tourism was much slower to develop. Back in 1861, William Grainge had forecast that the railway would quickly 'open out the district to the tourist and the health seeker, where they may roam at leisure amid the wildest mountain glens, and imbibe health and strength from the purest mountain breezes'. It did not happen. Hopes that Pateley Bridge might emulate Ilkley in neighbouring Wharfedale and become a flourishing spa town were doomed to disappointment, but few could then have sensed a massive development that was to bring a new era to both Nidderdale and its railway.

A thirsty Bradford

By the 1880s a straight-flying crow heading due south from Pateley Bridge for twenty miles might well decide to beat its wings and make a hasty retreat. Below and scarcely visible through a dense pall of black smoke was Bradford and its hundreds of mill chimneys. As wool capital of the world, the town had expanded at a meteoric rate with its population increasing from 67,000 in

1841 to 216,000 in 1891. It handled three-quarters of the West Riding's worsted trade, adopting the official motto 'Work Conquers All' and the unofficial 'Where there's muck there's money'.

Colossal amounts of water were needed to support such industrial expansion and it was soon clear that reservoir construction on a huge scale was the only option. In 1887 Bradford turned its attention to Upper Nidderdale and the outcome was three awesome projects that took half a century to complete and brought transformation in their wake. First off was Gouthwaite, a two-mile long compensation reservoir between Ramsgill and Wath necessary to satisfy those holding rights to take water from the Nidd. It was built between 1893 and 1901 by John Best & Son of Edinburgh, with stone being brought down to the dam by a standard-gauge railway incline on the east side of the valley. Horses rather than locomotives were used on the construction site.

With the compensation reservoir complete, work could start on the major part of the scheme to supply water to Bradford. The chosen location was Angram close to the headwaters of the Nidd. Ultimately holding 1.1 billion gallons of water, it was clear from the outset that a major problem was going to be its utter remoteness over a dozen miles from the nearest town of Pateley Bridge. When in 1900 it was decided to proceed with the project, it was sufficiently large to attract national interest. It came to the attention of the London-based Power & Traction Ltd, already active in the locality with proposals that proved abortive to build an electric railway from Ripon to Studley Royal to take visitors to Fountains Abbey. The company sensed an opportunity and in March 1901 obtained sanction to build a narrow gauge Nidd Valley Light Railway from Pateley Bridge to Lofthouse, half-way to Angram. It commenced land acquisition, but took no further action and in August 1903 the powers were purchased by Bradford Corporation for £2,000 [2016 = £194,000]. Tenders were now invited for construction of both the reservoir and the light railway – and three months later John Best became the successful bidder in both cases.

Narrow Gauge in Nidderdale

MEN and materials could with difficulty be brought up the twisting valley road to Lofthouse, from where a private road to the reservoir site had already been completed. John Best could therefore make an immediate start in building a steeply graded line alongside it. He opted for 3ft gauge, probably because of the ready availability of suitable contractors' locomotives and the fact that it was common in Ireland where he had recently undertaken major work on the Cork, Blackrock & Passage Railway.

Construction of the Nidd Valley Light Railway was delayed by a bureaucratic dispute with the Board of Trade, which was reluctant to create the precedent of a corporation building a light railway outside its own municipality. It was not until December 1903 that it gave formal approval, with borrowing powers of £30,000 [2016 = £3 million], on the understanding that a public passenger service would be provided. This enabled John Best to start on the required contractor's earthworks and extend the 3ft-gauge line south from Lofthouse all the way down to Pateley Bridge.

Running along the eastern shore of Gouthwaite Reservoir, it presented few engineering difficulties. The result was an impressive narrow gauge railway with an overall length of 12¾ miles, well in excess of such established and well-known undertakings as the Southwold and the Ravenglass & Eskdale. Yet it remains largely unknown to narrow gauge devotees. This is partly because it was a private line rather than a public railway but it also had the shortest of lives.

Its moment of greatest glory came in July 1904. South of Lofthouse it was not yet complete, but the line up to Angram was ready to receive the Lord Mayor of Bradford and his entourage. The civic party left the city in a special train for Pateley Bridge, from where they were taken up the dale by road to be greeted by the impressive sight of a train of fifteen navvy wagons with specially fitted seats. Double-headed to cope with the steep 1 in 40 gradients, it took the civic party up to the site of the dam for a sod-cutting ceremony followed by suitable refreshments. Sadly not ready for the great occasion was a saloon carriage, which the corporation had felt the need to order in February 1904. Low-slung and carried on four wheels, with the city arms on its sides, it had its own shed at Lofthouse. It ended its days with the saloon body being fitted to a standard gauge truck and delivered to the Wantage Tramway in Oxfordshire.

Despite this purchase, the early demise of the narrow gauge was imminent. During their celebratory visit the civic party paused at Gouthwaite on their outward journey to cut the first sod of the Nidd Valley Light Railway. Although it had been authorised as a narrow gauge line, there was now constant pressure from the North Eastern Railway, stressing that standard gauge would avoid all the costs and delays of transfers of goods. Their arguments won the day and the Board of Trade agreed that this alternative could be adopted.

The 3ft gauge remained in place to facilitate construction of the Light Railway, but it soon became mixed gauge all the way up to Angram. The section north of Lofthouse was adapted first and hence the adventurous decision taken to hitch a standard gauge locomotive behind a Foden steam wagon and tow it up the valley from Pateley Bridge. The engine's wheels cut deep into the road surface to the fury of the local police sergeant, but he failed to arrest the extraordinary cavalcade! By 1906 sections of what one visitor described as

Motive power headquarters of the Nidd Valley Light Railway at Pateley Bridge.
The water tower is an amazing contraption with all the appearance of an afterthought.
Outside the two-road shed are the railmotor and *Blythe*, an Avonside 0-6-0ST built
in 1922. Photomatic

'three-legged rail' were being pulled out and September 1907 brought the
formal opening of the Nidd Valley Light Railway. The era of the narrow gauge
had lasted less than four years.

Nidd Valley Light Railway

ONCE the first sod of the Nidd Valley Light Railway had been ceremonially cut
in July 1904, a dedicated corporation sub-committee took its responsibilities
seriously. It first decided to gain hints on working such a line by a series of
visits to the Vale of Rheidol, the Welshpool & Llanfair, the Tanat Valley and,
last but not least, the Kent & East Sussex managed by the redoubtable
Colonel Stephens.

Next on the agenda was the matter of rolling stock, where the Metropolitan
Railway came to the rescue following recent electrification. It was possible to
acquire two locomotives and ten coaches for the respective all-in prices of
£1,350 and £800 (the equivalent of about £115,000 and £72,000 today). The
two locomotives were a pair of the famous 4-4-0 side tanks built by Beyer
Peacock. Weighing up to 46½ tons they were decidedly heavy for the very light
track and their 5ft 10in. driving wheels were far from ideal for conditions in

Nidderdale. Yet they certainly added a note of distinction to the line with their Indian red livery and Bradford's coat of arms. Far from new, the oldest dating from 1866 became No.1 *Holdsworth* and its younger sister was No.2 *Milner.* The names were in recognition of two aldermen playing a leading role in the creation of the city's reservoirs.

The sub-committee did its job well and minimising expenditure was clearly not a prime consideration. At Pateley Bridge there was a completely separate two-platform terminus close to the sidings at the foot of Scot Gate Ash Quarry incline. The station had a signal-box equipped with Tyer's tablet equipment and beyond it was a carriage shed plus a two-road engine shed with coaling stage and water tower. Substantial two-storey buildings were provided at the other stations.

The September 1907 opening by Alderman J. Goodwin, Lord Mayor of Bradford, was another grand occasion with a four-coach train working through from Pateley Bridge to Angram. There had again been indulgence in the purchase of a special saloon carriage, which was included at the rear and stood out by virtue of its 'Bradford Corporation Nidd Valley' lettering and the city arms on the lower side of the body. At the reservoir site, John Best had brought civilisation to the mountain wilderness by creating a village that included 'superior bungalow residences' for such key figures as a doctor and a policeman, living huts for the workmen, a hospital, school, canteen, mission church and a reading room.

The civic party and numerous guests adjourned for a sumptuous five-course lunch complete with sherry, champagne, claret and brandy. So great was the celebration that the city's Temperance Council protested about the amount spent on 'intoxicating drinks'. It totalled more than £11,000 in today's money, but it was a fitting occasion to mark completion of the last railway to be built in the Dales. There was probably little concern that the total cost of constructing the Nidd Valley Light Railway had been way in excess of the borrowing powers of £30,000 authorised in 1903. It was a fair point that these costs had envisaged a narrow gauge line and the Board of Trade accordingly agreed to an increase to £66,000 [£6¼ million] in 1908. More interesting than the paperwork itself was the signature by its then president, Winston S. Churchill.

There were initially four trains each way between Pateley Bridge and Lofthouse in the summer and three in winter, timed to connect with arrivals and departures at the North Eastern station. An extra train was run on Wednesdays and Saturdays but there were no Sunday services. Despite much talk and hope, there were no through passenger workings between the two systems. The five-minute walk between the two terminals was not signposted

Heavy freights conveying construction materials to Angram and Scar House reservoirs must have been a stirring sight. In this 1928 scene, a lengthy train is being taken up the 1 in 40 bank north of Lofthouse by Hudswell Clarke 0-6-0T *Milner* and the 0-6-0ST *Blythe*. Two further locomotives are assisting at the rear. Photomatic / T.J. Edgington collection

and a great opportunity to develop tourism and excursion traffic was undoubtedly lost. Goods traffic saw wagons conveying materials for the reservoir being worked through Pateley Bridge by North Eastern Railway engines to the Light Railway sidings and then taken up to Angram by one of John Best's locomotives. A single engine was often insufficient north of Lofthouse and the most spectacular sight was heavy cement trains pounding up the steep gradients double-headed at the front and double-banked at the rear.

Work at Angram continued year by year but was greatly slowed down by the outbreak of World War I, which decimated the labour force. Although water first overflowed in January 1916, it was August 1917 before a certificate of

The ex Great Western Railway steam railmotor, built by Kerr Stuart in 1905 and acquired from a scrap merchant in 1921 to work most passenger services on the Nidd Valley Light Railway. It was named *Hill* in honour of Sir James Hill, a long-serving member of Bradford's waterworks committee. Author's collection

completion was issued. Construction traffic ceased and down at Pateley Bridge there was a noticeable reduction in rail activity, heightened by the closure of Scot Gate Ash Quarry. Nidd Valley Light Railway passenger services were now just three each way and there were real fears that the line would see a complete shut down. Yet once again events were to take a very different turn.

Largest of them all

IN 1921 Bradford decided to go ahead with Scar House Reservoir immediately downriver from Angram. It was to have double the capacity at 2.2 billion gallons and take even longer to complete. It also set a precedent by being built by direct labour, which immediately brought significant changes to rail access. The corporation was now in total control and north of Lofthouse there was in effect a goods-only extension of the Nidd Valley Light Railway rather than merely a contractor's line. The result was a series of improvements on this upper section, which had seen virtually no traffic for three years. Many curves were eased and the track improved, with two additional loops being provided. A major work was the creation of a 180yd tunnel cutting out a sharp curve at the point where Nidderdale swung abruptly through a ninety degree curve.

It was used by the heavily loaded ascending trains battling against the steep grade, whereas those going down dale empty continued to follow the original route.

Apart from materials being brought up to start reservoir construction, a priority was to create a village at Scar House. Housing a resident population of over a thousand, it was much larger than the former settlement at Angram with additional facilities including a concert hall, recreation room and a complete shopping centre boasting a grocer and fishmonger, butcher, hair dresser, boot repairer, post office and bank. Essentials arriving by train included coal from Garforth colliery, barrels of beer and potatoes for a fish & chip shop and flour for a bakery capable of producing 200 loaves per hour. The final touch was 110 volts D.C. electric lighting, which put the village way ahead of most Dales communities at this time. Summer days could occasionally be glorious but winters at over a thousand feet above sea level were often a matter of survival in the face of fierce blizzards and deep snow. On one occasion the village was isolated for weeks on end until an engine and goods wagon managed to force their way through to Pateley Bridge and return with vital food supplies.

Two engine sheds were built at Scar House to accommodate eleven loco-motives, used to handle incoming traffic and work on zig-zag railways leading down to the site of a dam that was 1,500ft long, 135ft wide and ultimately consumed a million tons of concrete. There was also a two-road shed built to house four-wheel carriages, bought from the Maryport & Carlisle Railway about 1922 to provide residents of Scar House with a means of escaping to civilisation. These services generally ran on Tuesdays and Thursdays for wives and families to go shopping and on Saturdays for the workmen, who spent their wages in the pubs of Pateley Bridge and were infamous for riotous behaviour on the return journey. Such trains normally worked only as far as Lofthouse, where a connection was made with the Nidd Valley Light Railway. Here passenger services were by now generally handled by an attractive steam railmotor built by Kerr Stuart in 1905 for the Great Western Railway.

The great day of the year in the late 1920s was always Nidderdale Show at Pateley Bridge when all and sundry from Scar House would mingle with crowds who had come up on what was now the LNER branch. Special cheap day returns were available from any station within a radius of 60 miles, thus attracting visitors from Bradford, Leeds and York. Cattle, fat sheep, gaudy swings and roundabouts came in by rail, and when it was all over the showmen would stagger into the station with sacks full of coins. The harassed booking clerk had to count up the cash and keep back the amount owing for carriage charges!

In 1930 there was a change in fortunes when public passenger and goods services on the Nidd Valley Light Railway were withdrawn and it became a

The desolate two-platform terminus of the NVLR at Pateley Bridge in July 1935, five years after it had seen its last passenger train. The goods shed is on the extreme left.
W.A. Camwell

private line with exactly the same status as the section above Lofthouse. It was now the dark days of the slump and there seemed no urgency to complete Scar House, probably because industrial activity was so reduced that Angram could meet all of Bradford's needs. The official opening finally took place in September 1936, the whole of the line then being lifted and a massive three-day sale of rolling stock, track and other equipment taking place in Pateley Bridge in June 1937. For the first time in almost fifty years there was no reservoir construction in the dale, which was now served solely by a typical branch line with little left to make it stand out from the crowd.

Final years

IF nothing else, the service up and down the branch was amazing in its consistency, as for 32 years it was worked by the same 0-4-4T No.1839, built in 1895. It had its own shed at Pateley Bridge, originally a stone structure but later rebuilt in wood, probably due to subsidence of the river bank. The shed accommodated just the one locomotive but employed two drivers, two firemen and a cleaner who worked alone at night. The engine was prepared for a morning train to Harrogate, generally leaving around 7.25am and then heading back up the dale for a second return working. After a layover at Starbeck shed for coal and water, it was back to Pateley Bridge again where the second crew

took over the afternoon services. On Saturdays one of the crews worked overtime on an additional evening train and on summer Sundays there was a trip to Leeds and back.

In 1939 the 0-4-4T was fitted to work a push-and-pull unit, which may have achieved some economies but failed to arrest a gradual decline. By 1950 there were just two trains each way with an additional working on Saturdays. The branch was earmarked as one of over a hundred forecast to close the following year and the fatal day came at the end of March 1951 when what was now G5 No.67253 worked the last passenger trains. It was a gloomy occasion, made worse by over an inch of rail falling within an hour.

A pick-up goods service continued but by the early 1960s it often comprised just two wagons. It was a sorry state of affairs that could not continue and the last train trundled up the branch in October 1964. There were local ideas of revival with a service operated by diesel multiple units, but in truth the population was just too small in the harsh realities of the Beeching age. Such optimistic hopes no doubt died the following spring when dieselisation failed to save the rail connection to the much larger town of Otley over the hill in lower Wharfedale. The West Riding County Council now put forward a scheme to make the disused trackbed from Ripley to Pateley Bridge into a footpath and linear park, but even this crumb of consolation died through opposition from landowners. After just over one hundred years it was the end of the railway age in Nidderdale.

Opposite, top: The afternoon train from Harrogate arrives at Pateley Bridge on 8 April 1950. A single carriage suggests that the writing was clearly on the wall and passenger services were withdrawn less than a year later. G5 0-4-4T No.67384 was standing in for No.67253, which was the branch engine for an amazing 32 years. T.J. Edgington

Lower: The sad sight at Pateley Bridge just prior to freight traffic ceasing in October 1964. It was hopelessly uneconomic with only an odd wagon or two to be collected by K1 2-6-0 No.62038. David Hey

Reference section

Opening dates of railways

	Line	Company at opening	From	To
10 September 1846	P+G	Y&N	Dalton junction (1)	Richmond
6 March 1848	P+G	YN&B	Northallerton	Leeming Lane
30 July 1849	P+G	NW	Skipton	Ingleton
1 February 1855	P+G	NE	Leeming Lane	Bedale
24 November 1855	G	B&L	Bedale	Leyburn
19 May 1856	P	B&L	Bedale	Leyburn
24 August 1861	G	L&C	Ingleton	Low Gil
16 September 1861	P	L&C	Ingleton	Low Gill
1 May 1862	P+G	NE	Ripley junction	Pateley Bridge
1 February 1865	P	NE	Arthington	Otley
1 August 1865	P	O&I	Otley	Ilkley
	P	Mid	Apperley junction	Burley junction
1 October 1866	G	NE	Arthington	Otley
	G	O&I	Otley	Ilkley
	G	Mid	Apperley junction	Burley junction
9 June 1875	P+G	NE	Melmerby	Masham
2 August 1875	G	Mid	Settle Junction	Carlisle
1 May 1876	P	Mid	Settle Junction	Carlisle
1 February 1877	P+G	NE	Leyburn	Askrigg
1 June 1878	P +G	NE	Askrigg	Hawes
1 October 1878	P+G	Mid	Hawes Junction (2)	Hawes
16 May 1888	P	Mid	Ilkley	Bolton Abbey
27 August 1888	G	Mid	Ilkley	Bolton Abbey
1 October 1888	P+G	Mid	Bolton Abbey	Skipton
29 July 1902	P+G	YD	Embsay junction	Grassington
11 September 1907	P+G	NVL	Pateley Bridge	Lofthouse

Column 3 shows the owning company at date of opening.

NOTES
(1) Renamed Eryholme junction 1901
(2) Renamed Garsdale 1932

Closure dates

	Line	Company at Grouping	From	To
1 January 1930	P+G	NVL	Pateley Bridge	Lofthouse
22 September 1930	P	YD	Embsay junction	Grassington
1 January 1931	P	NE	Melmerby	Masham
2 April 1951	P	NE	Ripley junction	Pateley Bridge
1 February 1954	P	Mid/LNW	Clapham	Low Gill (1)
26 April 1954	P	NE	Northallerton	Hawes (2)
16 March 1959	P+G	Mid	Garsdale	Hawes
11 November 1963	G	NE	Melmerby	Masham
27 April 1964	G	NE	Redmire	Hawes
31 October 1964	G	NE	Ripley junction	Pateley Bridge
22 March 1965	P	NE/O&IJt	Arthington	Burley junction
22 March 1965	P	Mid	Ilkley	Skipton (3)
5 July 1965	G	NE/O&IJt	Arthington	Burley junction
5 July 1965	G	Mid	Ilkley	Embsay junction
26 July 1966	G	Mid/LNW	Clapham	Low Gill
3 March 1969	P	NE	Eryholme junction	Richmond
	G	NE	Catterick Bridge	Richmond
11 August 1969	G	YD	Swinden Siding	Grassington
February 1970	G	NE	Eryholme junction	Catterick Bridge

Column 3 shows the owning company at Grouping on 1 January 1923.

NOTES

(1) Line retained as diversionary route and for school specials and excursions until complete closure on 26 July 1966.

(2) Reopened by Wensleydale Railway, Leeming Bar to Leyburn 4 July 2003; to Redmire 1 August 2004.

(3) Reopening of portion of line completed by Embsay & Bolton Abbey Steam Railway 1 May 1998.

Stations

Opening and closure dates to passengers

	Company	Opened	Closed
Addingham	Mid	16 May 1888	22 March 1965
Ainderby	YN&B6	March 1848	26 April 1954
Askrigg	NE	1 February 1877	26 April 1954
Aysgarth	NE	1 February 1877	26 April 1954
Barbon	L&C	16 September 1861	1 February 1954
Bedale	NE	1 February 1855	26 April 1954 (1)
Bell Busk	NW	30 July 1849	4 May 1959
Ben Rhydding	O&IJ	1 August 1865 (2)	
Birstwith	NE	1 May 1862	2 April 1951
Bolton Abbey	Mid	16 May 1888	22 March 1965 (3)
Burley	O&IJ	1 August 1865	
Catterick Bridge	Y&N	10 September 1846	3 March 1969
Clapham	NW	30 July 1849	
Constable Burton	B&L	19 May 1856	26 April 1954
Crakehall	B&L	19 May 1856	26 April 1954
Dacre	NE	1 May 1862	2 April 1951
Darley	NE	February 1864	2 April 1951
Dent	Mid	6 August 1877 (4)	
Embsay	Mid	1 October 1888	22 March 1965 (5)
Finghall Lane	B&L	19 May 1856	26 April 1954 (6)
Gargrave	NW	30 July 1849	
Garsdale	Mid	1 August 1876 (4) (7)	
Giggleswick	NW	30 July 1849 (8)	
Grassington	YD	29 July 1902	22 September 1930
Hampsthwaite	NE	September 1866	2 January 1950
Hawes	Mid/NE	1 June 1878	16 March 1959
Hellifield	NW	30 July 1849	
Horton-in-Ribblesdale	Mid	1 May 1876 (4)	
Ilkley	O&IJ	1 August 1865	
Ingleton	Mid	30 July 1849 (9)	1 February 1954
Ingleton	L&C	16 September 1861	1 January 1917
Jervaulx	B&L	19 May 1856 (10)	26 April 1954
Kirkby Lonsdale	L&C	16 September 1861	1 February 1954
Leeming Bar	YN&B	6 March 1848 (11)	26 April 1954 (1)
Leyburn	B&L	19 May 1856	26 April 1954 (1)
Lofthouse-in-Nidderdale	NVL	12 September 1907	1 January 1930
Long Preston	NW	30 July 1849	
Masham	NE	10 June 1875	1 January 1931
Middleton-on-Lune	L&C	16 September 1861	13 April 1931
Moulton	Y&N	10 September 1846	3 March 1969
Pateley Bridge	NE 1	May 1862	2 April 1951
Pateley Bridge	NVL	12 September 1907	1 January 1930

Pool	NE	1 February 1865	22 March 1965
Ramsgill	NVL	12 September 1907	1 January 1930
Redmire	NE	1 February 1877	26 April 1954 (12)
Ribblehead	Mid	4 December 1876 (4)	
Richmond	Y&N	10 September 1846	3 March 1969
Ripley Valley	NE	1 May 1862 (13)	2 April 1951
Rylstone	YD	30 July 1902	22 September 1930
Scorton	Y&N	10 September 1846	3 March 1869
Scruton	YN&B	January 1857	26 April 1954 (14)
Sedbergh	L&C	16 September 1861	1 February 1954
Settle	Mid	1 May 1876	
Settle Junction	Mid	2 October 1876	1 November 1877
Skipton	L&B	8 September 1847	
Spennithorne	NE	September 1863	26 April 1954
Tanfield	NE	10 June 1875	1 January 1931
Wath-in-Nidderdale	NVL	12 September 1907	1 January 1930
Wensley	NE	1 February 1877	26 April 1954

Column 2 shows the owning company at the date of opening.

NOTES

(1) Reopened by Wensleydale Railway 4 July 2003
(2) Initially private station; public opening 1 July 1866
(3) Reopened by Embsay & Bolton Abbey Steam Railway 1 May 1998
(4) Closed 4 May 1970, fully reopened 14 July 1986
(5) Reopened by Yorkshire Dales Railway 19 May 1979
(6) Reopened as Finghall by Wensleydale Railway 23 December 2004
(7) Opened 1876 as Hawes Junction; renamed Garsdale 1932
(8) Opened 1849 as Settle; renamed Giggleswick 1877
(9) Closed 1 June 1850; reopened 1 October 1861
(10) Opened 1856 as Newton-le-Willows; renamed Jervaulx 1887
(11) Opened 1848 as Leeming Lane; renamed Leeming Bar 1902
(12) Reopened by Wensleydale Railway 1 August 2004
(13) Opened 1862 as Killinghall; renamed Ripley 1862 and Ripley Valley 1875
(14) Formally reopened by Wensleydale Railway 22 November 2014

Minor changes in station names are not detailed.

Abbreviations

P	Passengers
G	Goods
B&L	Bedale & Leyburn Railway
L&B	Leeds & Bradford Railway
L&C	Lancaster & Carlisle Railway
LNW	London & North Western Railway
Mid	Midland Railway
NE	North Eastern Railway
NVL	Nidd Valley Light Railway
NW	North Western Railway
O&I	Otley & Ilkley Joint Railway
Y&N	York & Newcastle Railway
YN&B	York, Newcastle & Berwick Railway

Further reading

General

Gordon Biddle, *Britain's Historic Railway Buildings* (Oxford University Press, 2003)

Michael Blakemore, *Railways of the Yorkshire Dales* (Atlantic, 2001)

Bill Fawcett, *A History of North Eastern Railway Architecture* (North Eastern Railway Association, 3 vols, 2001–5)

K. Hoole, *Railways in the Yorkshire Dales* (Dalesman, 1975)

K. Hoole, *A Regional History of the Railways of Great Britain, Vol. 4 The North East* (David & Charles, 1974)

David Joy, *A Regional History of the Railways of Great Britain, Vol. 8 South and West Yorkshire* (David & Charles, 1984)

Michael Quick, *Railway Passenger Stations in Great Britain: A Chronology* (Railway & Canal Historical Society, 2002)

W.W. Tomlinson, *The North Eastern Railway – its rise and development* (2nd ed. David & Charles, 1967)

Wharfedale

Martin Bairstow, *Railways through Airedale and Wharfedale* (Author, 2004)

Peter E. Baughan, *The Railways of Wharfedale* (David & Charles, 1969)

Donald Binns, *The Yorkshire Dales Railway – The Grassington Branch* (Northern Heritage, 1990)

David Joy, 'Rails through Ilkley' (in *Backtrack*, Vol.29, No.4, April 2015)

David Joy, 'Rails to Grassington' (in *Backtrack*, Vol.25, No.5, May 2011)

David Joy, *Yorkshire Dales Railway* (Dalesman, 1983)

F.W. Smith & Martin Bairstow, *The Otley and Ilkley Joint Railway* (Author, 1992)

Ribblesdale, Dentdale and Garsdale

V.R. Anderson & G.K. Fox, *Stations and Structures of the Settle & Carlisle Railway* (Oxford Publishing, 1986)

Peter E. Baughan, *North of Leeds – the Leeds–Settle–Carlisle line and its branches* (Roundhouse, 1966)

Frederick W. Houghton & W. Hubert Foster, *The Story of the Settle-Carlisle Line* (Norman Arch, 1948)

David Jenkinson, *Rails in the Fells* (Peco, 1973)

W.R. Mitchell, *Thunder in the Mountains – The men who built Ribblehead* (Great Northern, 2009)

W.R. Mitchell & David Joy, *Settle–Carlisle Railway* (Dalesman, nine editions from 1966)

Martin Pearson, *The Settle Carlisle Railway 1850–1990 – The Building and Saving of a Great Railway* (Author, 2016)

Bob Swallow, *Against the Grade – Working on the Settle–Carlisle Railway* (Great Northern, 2011)

Frederick S. Williams, *The Midland Railway: its rise and progress* (Straham, 1876)

Swaledale

Bill Fawcett, *George Townsend Andrews of York – 'The Railway Architect'*
(York Architectural & York Archaeological Society & North Eastern Railway Association,
2011)

R. Fieldhouse & B. Jennings, *A History of Richmond and Swaledale* (Phillimore, 1978)

A.J. Ludlam, *The Catterick Camp Military Railway and the Richmond Branch*
(Oakwood Press, 1993)

Wensleydale

Christine Hallas, *The Wensleydale Railway* (Great Northern, 2004)

Stanley C. Jenkins, *The Wensleydale Branch* (Oakwood Press, 2002)

David Joy, *Guide to the Wensleydale Railway* (Great Northern, 2005)

David Joy, 'Rails in Wensleydale' (in *Backtrack*, Vol.27, No.4, April 2013)

Masham and Colsterdale

Harold D. Bowtell, *Lesser Railways of the Yorkshire Dales – and the dam builders in the age of steam*
(Plateway Press, 1991)

'Reynardine', 'Rural and Obscure – Some Notes on the Masham Branch of the NER'
(in *Railway Bylines*, Vol.1, No.1, December 1995/January 1996)

Nidderdale

Harold D. Bowtell *(see above)*

D.J. Croft, *The Nidd Valley Light Railway* (Oakwood Press, 1987)

Bernard Jennings (ed.), *A History of Nidderdale* (Advertiser Press, 1967)

David Joy, 'Rails in Nidderdale' (in *Backtrack*, Vol.28, No.5, May 2014)

INDEX

Great Western Railway 84
Greenhow Hill 77
Green, T. & Son 74
Greta, river 13
Guiseley 10, 21, 31, 32
Gunpowder 43

Hack Fall 72
Hague, William 24
Hardraw Force 63
Harrogate 10, 21, 30, 31, 72, 75, 76, 85
Hartlepool 63
Hawes 17, 21, 43, 50, 62–64, 68, 70, 71
Hawes Junction 17, 43, 59, 63
Hellifield 43, 45
Helwith Bridge 40
Heysham 30, 31
Hoffmann kiln 39
Horses 43
Horton-in-Ribblesdale 15, 38, 54
Hudson, George 7, 11, 55, 59
Hudswell Clarke 58
Hunslet Engine Co. 74
Hydropathy 26, 29

Ilkley 10, 19, 21, 23, 25–28, 29–33, 35, 39, 72, 77
Ingleborough 40
Ingleton 12, 13, 14, 15, 21, 22, 39, 40, 42, 46
Inverness 48

Jaques & Co. 58
Jervaulx 70

Keighley 11
Kent & East Sussex Railway 80
Kerr Stuart 58, 84
King's Lynn 58
Kirkby Lonsdale 12
Kirkby Stephen 15
Knaresborough 75

Lancashire & Yorkshire North Eastern Railway 25
Lancaster 12, 13, 14, 39
Lancaster & Carlisle Railway 12, 14
Langcliffe 39
Leeds 10, 11, 14, 18, 21, 28–33, 37, 48, 50, 51, 72, 84
Leeds & Bradford Railway 11, 13
Leeds & Liverpool Canal 11
Leeds & Thirsk Railway 10, 17, 25, 72, 75, 77
Leeming Bar 8, 24, 59, 60, 70, 71
Leyburn 5, 8, 10, 17, 18, 24, 56, 60, 64, 66, 70, 71, 72
Light Railways 20, 24, 78–85
Liverpool, Manchester & Newcastle-upon-Tyne Junction Railway 18
Lockington 59
Lofthouse 20, 78, 79, 81, 83, 84, 85
London 10, 13, 30, 46, 48, 58, 77
London & North Eastern Railway 31, 66, 84
London & North Western Railway 12, 14, 15
London, Midland & Scottish Railway 22, 45, 48

Lothersdale 38
Low Gill 13, 14, 21, 42, 46

McAlpine, Sir William 24
Malham Tarn 33
Manchester 18, 19, 30, 33, 50, 63
Maryport & Carlisle Railway 84
Masham 5, 17, 20, 21, 72–74
Melmerby 17, 72
Metcalfe, George 75, 76, 77
Metropolitan Railway 80
Midland Railway 6, 10–17, 19, 20, 22, 26, 27, 30, 33, 40, 45, 59, 62, 66, 68
Mitchell, David 53
Morecambe 31, 36, 40, 64
Morrison, Walter 33, 35

Nafferton 59
Narrow gauge lines 38, 72, 74, 78–80
Navvies 43
Newcastle 18, 19, 21, 33, 63, 75
Newcastle & Darlington Junction Railway 7
Newport-on-Tees 31
Nidd Bridge 75, 77
Nidderdale 5, 10, 20, 75–87
Nidd, river 10, 72, 75
Nidd Valley Light Railway 5, 20, 78–85
Northallerton 7, 17, 18, 21, 22, 24, 59, 61, 62, 63, 64, 66, 72
North Eastern Railway 6–10, 17, 20, 26, 30, 31, 59–63, 66, 72–74, 75–77, 82
North London Railway 58
North Western Railway 14, 39
North Yorkshire Moors Railway 75
Norwich 66

Omnibuses, horse-drawn 25, 27, 75
Otley 10, 21, 25, 27, 28, 30–33, 87
Otley & Ilkley Joint Railway 10, 26–28
Ouse, river 75
Overend Gurney 15

Pateley Bridge 5, 10, 20, 21, 72, 75–79, 81–85, 87
Penyghent 39
Plews, Nathaniel 56
Pool 32
Portable Buildings Company 35
Portillo, Michael 22
Power & Traction Ltd 78
Preston 50
Princetown 62
Prosser, Thomas 61, 75
Pullman cars 48
Push-and-pull trains 87

QUARRIES
  Arcow 54; Craven 39; Dry Rigg 54; Harmby 68; Hawbank 23; Helwith Bridge 40; Horton 38, 40; Ingleton 54; Lofthouse 77; Pateley Bridge 10, 77, 81, 83; Redmire 22, 24, 68, 70, 71; Skirethornes 38; Swinden 23, 24, 38; Wensley 68